THE RECOVERED VOICE

THE RECOVERED VOICE

Tales of Practical Psychotherapy

Rainer Matthias Holm-Hadulla

KARNAC

First published in German as *Integrative Psychotherapie: Zwölf exemplarische Geschichten aus der Praxis*

First published in English in 2017 by
Karnac Books Ltd
118 Finchley Road, London NW3 5HT

Copyright © 2015 Klett-Cotta - Cottas'che, Buchhandlung Nachfolger GmbH, Stuttgart.
English translation by Andrew Jenkins

British Library Cataloguing in Publication Data

A C.I.P. for this book is available from the British Library

ISBN 978 1 78220 398 8

Edited, designed and produced by The Studio Publishing Services Ltd
www.publishingservicesuk.co.uk
e-mail: studio@publishingservicesuk.co.uk

www.karnacbooks.com

CONTENTS

ACKNOWLEDGEMENTS

I should like to express my profound gratitude to all the patients featuring in this book. With their trusting and creative cooperation, they have enabled me to arrive at the therapeutic model and the treatment strategies we have been discussing here. In addition, they have assessed the therapy they have undergone from their own personal perspectives and granted me the permission to publish their stories. With their generosity, they have given all those with an interest in psychotherapy valuable insights into the way it works in practice.

Rainer Matthias Holm-Hadulla is a professor of psychotherapeutic medicine at the University of Heidelberg and a training analyst in the International Psychoanalytic Association. He also teaches at various psychotherapeutic training institutions. For decades, he has been at the head of a team of psychotherapists with very different backgrounds: humanistic, cognitive–behavioural, systemic, psychoanalytic, and existential. Visiting professorships have taken him to China and South America, and he has been elected a member of numerous interdisciplinary research bodies. His main academic (and practical) interests focus on creativity in all its various forms.

Introduction: existential creativity

Creativity is the essence of life. This is not only true of art, music, and drama: everyday life is a creative challenge. Even babies will transform sensations from their interior and exterior world into new and usable forms. In the process, the brain develops, the psyche gains coherence, and the spirit flourishes. All the way up to high old age, it makes all the difference whether we are inspired by the fragrance of our morning tea to reflect on a dream and to remember the shining eyes of a person we love. Yet, we all know that the creative encounter with the world might have its obstacles. Sometimes, we need help to (re)discover our personal abilities and social potential.

Creativity, in itself, is ambivalent. It offers us supreme felicity, but might also be bound up with sadness and despair. Aphrodite (Venus in Latin), the goddess of beauty and fruitfulness, is one incarnation of the ambivalence of creativity. Her father, the "creator-god" Uranos, can no longer bear the fruitfulness of his wife Gaia, the "earth-mother". Hesiod describes how he sets about killing all his children until Gaia persuades her youngest son, Kronos, to fight his father. With a sickle given to him by his mother, he castrates Uranos and throws his bleeding genitals into the sea. The bloody foam gives birth to Aphrodite (Venus), the goddess of beauty and fertility. In their later careers, these goddesses engender not only undiluted bliss but also profound despair. In that seminal document of Western culture, the *Iliad*, Aphrodite is partly responsible for the devastating Trojan War. In my book, *Creativity between Construction and Destruction*, I have shown that nearly every culture conceives of creativity as a struggle between constructive and destructive forces. This struggle also takes place in people's individual lives.

Every human being has to negotiate a path between constructive and destructive forces. In this, most are given the assistance they need by parents and friends, as well as by teachers, colleagues, and counsellors. Religious, philosophical, and experiential wisdom also guides us. Thus, in all cultures, we find wise persons helping questing individuals to find their own way. In the modern age, psychotherapists are among those who have not only taken it upon themselves to cure disorders, but also to act as existential companions. They assist their patients in using their individual and social resources to find a path to individual well-being and social responsibility. As we shall see, this task is a creative challenge.

The following twelve narratives referring to persons with typical psychic problems and disorders are intended to exemplify how modern psychotherapy works. First, there is the singer Saskia, who "nearly dies" after separation from her lover: "I've lost my voice". Student Klara suffers from diffuse anxieties and nagging jealousy. She isolates herself and feels increasingly disgruntled. Then there is the aspiring economist who fails his final examination. He is no longer able to immerse himself in the computer games that blot out "all earthly things". The pianist Maria is reluctant to display her talents because that makes her "irrationally vulnerable". She retreats from the stage and lapses into a spiral of self-depreciation and guilt feelings. The successful young doctor Monika feels unfulfilled and depressed and has the impression that she "is standing beside herself". Always busy around the house, Hilde is not happy with her marriage and becomes a permanent fixture in her doctors' waiting-rooms: "Everything hurts." John, a young lawyer, wants to be perfect and wonders why he has such a hard time of it: "I always create conflicts and have no idea why." Student Christian cannot stand the dullness of everyday life and constantly looks for "excitement and glamour". He is unable to work and neglects his gifts and talents. Richard, a successful architect, feels null and void without "torrid sexual affairs". After ten years of marriage, his wife has just left him "for no apparent reason". He feels the impulse to shoot himself. A clerk who likes to be called Wolf feels devalued by a structural reform in his company: "They have pulled away the ground from under my feet." He is deeply offended and reacts with a long depressive phase. Musician Berthold seeks excitement and ecstasy but ends up in chaos. He is looking for a path between the Scylla of the unimaginative and the Charybdis of over-stimulation, a quest that has led to "psychotic breakdown". For years, student Mara has felt emotionally unstable and intellectually con-fused. Her relationships always end in violent altercations: "Should I do what my girlfriend did and escape this chaotic world by killing myself?" It will take a long course of therapy to enable her to under-stand herself and her relationships.

The text is structured by the most relevant diagnoses arrived at in psychotherapy. First, we witness the counselling process for a patient suffering from an adjustment disorder (Saskia). Then I describe the relatively brief treatments required in cases of mild depression and social anxiety (Klara, Joachim, Maria). There follow people who are suffering from moderate depression or from personality disorders (Maria, Hilda, Johann, Chris, Richard). Then we have the long and complex course of psychotherapy required for a patient with a life-threatening "severe depression" (Wolf). Subsequently, I describe inte-grative psychotherapy for a patient diagnosed as "schizophrenic" (Berthold). Finally, I report on psychoanalysis for a patient diagnosed with a "borderline personality disorder" (Mara). Mostly several years after completion of treatment, all these patients entered into a catam-nestic exchange with me, in which they rated their treatment them-selves. Their criticisms and confirmations have made this book possible. Some of the depicted patients wanted to read my version of the treatment they had received and made very valuable comments.

The individual case reports are designed to highlight the follow-ing aspects: how does a therapeutic relationship develop? What role does behaviour change play? How are dysfunctional opinions and beliefs corrected? How do unconscious conflicts come to the fore and how can they be resolved? How are creative self-realisation and social engagement reinforced? Central to the engagement with all these questions is an integrative treatment approach that is given theoreti-cal substantiation in the final chapter of this book. The therapeutic process begins with the establishment of a secure therapeutic alliance

(A), going on from there to integrate behavioural (B), cognitive (C), and psychodynamic/psychoanalytic (D) dimensions. Concern for these elements and their mutual interaction is part and parcel of psychotherapeutic practice as it is understood here. It springs from a basic attitude that sees understanding, communication, and creativity as the fundamentals of human existence (E).

TWELVE EXEMPLARY CASES

Stress reaction with anxiety and depression: a singer loses her voice

"It was a trauma for my self-confidence"

A conference on psychiatry and psychotherapy in Berlin. The building cool and functional, the usual comings and goings: speakers striding to their next venue, interested psychiatrists, psychotherapists, and psychologists hurrying from one talk to the next. The reception is nice enough, wine and finger-food, small talk, all vaguely boring. Back at the hotel, I check through my emails. One of them is a surprise: "I do apologise for bothering you, but I'm a singer and I've lost my voice. I feel awful. Can you give me an appointment?" Her name is Saskia and the mail gives me a pretty full account of the unhappiness and despair she is labouring under. She has read one of my books and hopes I can help her find her way back to herself. Normally, I never see patients outside my rooms, but in this case I make an exception and suggest that we meet the next morning at a nearby café. "Great!" she answers. "I never thought it would work! 11 a.m. at the café."

We recognise each other immediately: she is a slim, rather melancholy looking woman. We say hello and it strikes me how wan she looks, how limp her handshake is. We find a secluded corner and, in a downcast voice, she tells me her story: "I spent six years singing in small theatres in southern Germany before I came to Berlin. I had great hopes, but the reason why I came here was my boyfriend and the relationship folded almost immediately. My boyfriend said he intended to 'play the field' and I couldn't stand for that, so I gave him the push. Now I have this inflammation of the vocal cords, I can hardly speak above a whisper. It's as if all the zest has gone out of life. This trauma has ruined my confidence. So I'm all set for depression with subsequent suicide, right? But there's no way you can do it tastefully without getting other people involved." This flash of sarcastic humour is gone as quickly as it came. Gloom is all pervasive. "I loved him and now there's no hope for me." Saskia goes on to describe her disappointment and her bouts of depression in some detail. As I listen, I start feeling pretty disconsolate myself. My good mood has taken a nose dive; the coffee tastes like dishwater. "Alexander was Mister Right, but not on those conditions! Now my voice has gone! What am I to do? I practise every day, I want to communicate with my audiences, get back out there on stage. But there's no point."

I have no spontaneous ideas about how I can help her. My mind refuses to work. After a while, I remind myself of my duty as a therapist and tell myself I must find a solution or at least give Saskia a modicum of hope. However, given the state of despair she is in, I do not really see how this can be done just by talking to one another. My own helplessness starts to torment me. All I can think of is futile advice that would never help anyone, let alone Saskia. Yet, there is a kind of resonance between us, although I cannot define it more closely.

Saskia goes on talking at length about what she's been through. Suddenly, I remember Thomas Quasthoff, the famous singer. In the tearooms of a hotel, he once told me what a hard time he had as a child. As a thalidomide victim, he had been sent to some rather soulless children's home for treatment and felt dreadfully lonely and distressed. In search of solace, he took to moving his head back and forth rhythmically, but, unlike many other victims of the same condition, he did not bang his head against the wall but started to emit sounds. Later, when dark moods befell him, his singing teacher would say, "Put it all into the music!" I tell Saskia about this episode and suggest that she might like to sing more for herself rather than for an imaginary audience. She finds this worth thinking about. "Maybe it's a good idea to forget the others and try to feel myself more," she says. We then discuss a few techniques she can use to counteract a depressive crisis: reassuring everyday rituals, carrying on with one's work, getting plenty of exercise. If friends offer their support, I advise her to accept it. She does not want medication, but if her depression gets worse, I might have to give her something all the same.

Towards the end of our meeting, she tells me about an exchange she had with two girlfriends. The conclusion the women came to was that with a childhood like hers, there was very little chance of things coming to a good end. She had a "defect", and that was that. I ask her what they meant by all this and she tells me that immediately after her birth her mother had succumbed to an attack of depression that ultimately lasted several years: "She just wasn't there." As she says this, I am suddenly struck by the vital, attractive side of her personality. More or less on the spur of the moment, I say, "Of course that's very difficult for a small child. But at least you had her for nine months." She looks at me incredulously, then her eyes veil over and she smiles wanly: "That's a nice thought," she says.

Before we part, we run through anti-depressive behaviour strategies and arrange an appointment one week later via Skype. I am very keen to see how she is. Sometimes, one is surprised how quickly people recover, but what usually happens is that the symptoms stand out more starkly and intensive psychotherapy is the next stage.

Three days later, there is an email for me: "I'm sorry it's taken so long, but I want to tell you how sincerely grateful I am. Our meeting was so valuable and beneficial, much of what you said has been resonating in my mind ever since. Yesterday was my first 'ritual' and it was very emotional and fulfilling. If it didn't sound so twee, I'd say, 'You've relit the candle!'"

Reading the mail, my feelings are mixed. One the one hand, I am flattered, of course, but I do not believe in miracle healings. Purely rationally, I can say that the contact between us is good and that Saskia has become more optimistic. This is always the first step, and she has also shown that she can relate to my behaviour suggestions. Even more important is the fact that somehow we have reached an "understanding". The next few cases will show how difficult understanding each other can be but we will also see how gratifying it is when psychotherapy succeeds in triggering creative processes.

Two weeks later, Saskia Skypes me to say that she goes running regularly and that it does her good. "Dutifully" she has followed my advice and accepted a number of invitations from acquaintances. However, the best thing is that she has actually managed to sing for herself: "Odd, they were all sad songs, but somehow they helped me." In particular, a setting of Goethe's "Wonne der Wehmut" [Joy of Melancholy] had started her thinking. The poem says that one must give oneself up to pain in order to overcome it. "Is that really true?" she asks. My impression is that the sadness is still there, but she is facing up to it more actively.

Two weeks later, we talk on the phone. This time, the subject of death is uppermost in her mind. She has not yet got over her father's death last year. Now she has a clearer feeling for the strain that involves. As she engages with the matter, she suddenly begins to hope "that he might return as a friendly inner companion." She has started keeping a diary again and says, "That way, everything takes on a physical form." I find this difficult to understand, also I feel that Skyping does not really put us in touch with one another. She does not find it so distracting and continues with a detailed account of her thoughts and feelings. Finally, she thanks me for my patience.

At our next Skype encounter, Saskia is once again concerned with sorrowful experiences. She feels that she comes into her own when she can find musical expression for the pain of love. Her daily routine at her desk does her good and she is glad that she has taken my advice and continued to go about her daily chores. She has also yielded to my "gentle pressure" to go out and meet friends. She feels that she is capable of "dragging herself out of this swamp by the hair". She tells me that she has been through a deep, dark valley and believes her perception of herself has improved.

Three months after our first meeting, Saskia has found a new boy-friend, who "really does me good." But that is only possible "because I have found myself again." Rather doubtfully, she asks, "For how long?" Three months later again, she writes me a letter. Inspired by our conversations, she has thought much about her sadness and her fear of life. Interesting images from her childhood have suddenly reappeared. She has found out that the fear of "showing" her voice has to do with the unfeeling drill her stepfather exposed her to. When she sang badly, he criticised her; when she sang well, nothing was said. Her mother kept herself to herself; probably the situation was too much for her.

In her new life, much has changed. After initial hesitation, she gave ear to the overtures of her "dream partner" and is happy: "He freed me from my hedge of thorns like Sleeping Beauty and woke me from my ugly sleep." Something of fundamental significance has occurred: "I have found myself and my voice." At present, the relationship with this man is more important for her than her artistic development. One apparently paradoxical thing is that she now has fewer inhibitions about singing. She resolves never to do anything without mindfulness and love.

What was it about that brief period of psychotherapeutic counselling that helped Saskia? From the viewpoint of the ABCDE model outlined in the final chapter, we can summarise her progress as follows. A trusting relationship established itself spontaneously (A). Respect, interest and empathy were the basic conditions enabling Saskia to talk about her sufferings. Perhaps mutual admiration was a factor. Saskia found my book inspiring; I have always been an admirer of the singer's art. More importantly, we understood each other emotionally. However, the understanding resonance between us soon collapsed into itself and a gloomy mood ensued. This was only dispersed when we explored paths towards a solution at other levels.

Saskia was able to act upon my behavioural advice (B). With my encouragement, she felt able to actively reorganise her everyday life. She was more concerned to achieve a balanced rhythm. At the same time, she took issue with her avoidance mechanisms, exposing herself to social contacts, albeit reluctantly.

However, this was only feasible after her negative thought-loops had lost some of their force (C). Why did that happen? I believe that, in our exchanges, we intuitively developed new and meaningful perspectives that I was able to perceive and express on her behalf. Probably Saskia's stories and her body language (movement, facial expression, tone of voice) produced impressions that reminded me of the ideas I have described: for instance, the memory of Thomas Quasthoff or the idea that at least she had been at one with her mother for nine months. Ideas like that are not contained in teaching manuals, and I had never hit upon them before. Yet, in this specific encounter, they were highly significant.

In psychotherapeutic encounters, creative ideas usually materialise spontaneously when both partners are willing and able to give rein to their fantasies. They are in no way irrational. Although they are usually unconscious, they are rational and emotional responses to experiences. They can also be verified. For example, if the patient can relate to the therapist's ideas and new perspectives open up, one can be fairly sure that a productive dialogue has come about. Usually, unconscious relationship conflicts reveal themselves in spontaneous memories and fantasies. They may often be linked with life experiences of significance for the present. This is the psychodynamic and psychoanalytic level (D) which, like all the other dimensions of the ABCDE model, is described in detail in the final chapter.

Naturally, profound and far-reaching conflicts cannot be worked through in one psychotherapeutic session. Yet, as with Saskia, one can sometimes set in train an internal process in the course of which patients become more mindful of themselves. Some months after our encounter, Saskia wrote to me saying that she frequently recalled essential events from her past and, thus, was in a position to better understand her feelings and anxieties. At the session itself, Saskia had unconsciously given me access to fantasies that she herself could no longer entertain. This gave rise to solution-orientated ideas that I passed on to her, which, in its turn, helped her to perceive her own resources more clearly. Ultimately, this creative process plays a crucial part in any kind of counselling or psychotherapy (E).

Psychotherapeutic fundamentals described briefly in this narrative will be elaborated on in the following case reports.

Adjustment disorder: a medical student suffers from crippling jealousy

"I'm down and out"

K lara, a twenty-four-year-old medical student, has been suffering from massive insomnia for two to three months. She has a diffuse sense of anxiety and feels permanently out of sorts. In the night, she wakes up bathed in sweat and is "down and out". Her thoughts revolve around exam questions. She believes that her complaints are connected with the stress involved in preparing for her first-part finals in medicine.

The second major problem she describes is crippling jealousy. This, too, stops her from sleeping. Frequently, she thinks of her boyfriend's female acquaintances, compares herself with them, and finds it almost impossible to free herself of her self-doubts. She finds pretty brunettes with brown eyes and large breasts particularly dangerous rivals because these women are more erotically seductive than she is: "Why should my boyfriend resist?" She finds herself less attractive, there are many things about her that she dislikes: "a bit too big, breasts too small, blond hair". Sometimes, she makes an exhaustive attempt to find the reasons for her jealousy, mustering other women "almost obsessively" to find out what is seductive about their gestures and alluring about their physical appearance.

Klara wants professional success but is diffident about setting herself off from her boyfriend. She admires his intelligence and diligence and feels "hopelessly" inferior. My feeling is that, for some obscure reason, she is hiding behind her friend. At first, I find it difficult to understand why this attractive and appealing young woman should be so timid and forlorn. I ask myself, with a degree of anticipation, whether I will be able to accompany her on the path back to herself. The impression I have of her is that she is both trustful and resigned: "I don't know what's blocking me and whether anyone can help me."

Asked about her general situation, she tells me that she is in the ninth term of her medical studies and has been living with her boyfriend for nine months. He is also a medical student, just starting out on the preparations for the third part of his finals and always one step ahead of her. He is very successful, and this increases the pressure to which she subjects herself. Her own studies were interrupted by an intestinal disorder that took a long time to diagnose accurately. Cancer could not be ruled out. Finally, the doctors gave her anti-phlogistic medication. Despite the success of this treatment, the illness was still hanging over her "like a shadow". Klara has a variety of hobbies: she likes reading novels and (before her intestinal issues) was a serious tennis player.

Klara begins the account of her life by saying that "basically" she had a happy childhood. Her parents were very caring, particularly her "mummy". Sometimes, however, she thinks her mother might have been too anxious and careful. In the later course of treatment, she remembers that the married life of her parents had been adversely affected by an affair her father had with his secretary. Her mother had studied law and works in her father's legal firm. Her father is very successful, extremely active, and invariably cheerful: "He takes an interest in everything." Her sister is three years younger and their relationship is marked by intense rivalry: "We get on well but there's always this stupid competition between us." Her sister is studying to be a singer and is "fortunate enough to have a boyfriend who's a good pianist."

After her harmonious childhood, puberty brought extremely violent disagreements with her father: "He did everything he could to hold on to me." Her mother stayed in the background and tried to mediate between them. In the recent past and in the wake of her intestinal disorder, her relationship with her father has improved. She separated from her first boyfriend after three and a half years because he was either unwilling or unable to relate to the way she was developing.

In the therapeutic relationship, Klara initially appears eloquent and confident. She is at pains to be adult and self-assured, underlining this with the costume she has elected to wear and her formal manners. However, when she starts talking about her difficulties, this impression fades away. She appears timid and anxious, her voice is very quiet, and she seems more like an intimidated little girl. It looks as if she is unable to trust her femininity and feels that she is merely playing the role of a self-assured adult woman. My feelings and the fantasies she triggers in me are in accord with this verdict. On the one hand, I experience her as a confident and active young woman who has been temporarily disadvantaged by illness but who is otherwise in complete control of her life. On the other, the image I have of her in my mind's eye is that of an anxious, intimidated, and despondent little girl who has lost faith in her capacity for change.

We agree on a brief course of therapy comprising twenty-five sessions, which Klara finds rather lengthy. In view of her emotional and intellectual flexibility, the prospects of improving her behavioural blockades and pessimistic attitudes within this relatively short space of time appear to be good. I also expect to be able to address the autonomy/dependence conflicts that she is not yet consciously aware of. Finally, I feel justified in hoping that she will become more familiar with her creative potentialities.

In the sessions, Klara initially displays a vulnerable, needy, and anaclitic side. In her studies, she is still anything but self-reliant and has little confidence in her abilities. I try to provide active support by emphasising her strengths. She is quite willing to accept advice on how she might organise her work more effectively. We also talk about her cultural interests. Her response to this is positive, her concentration improves, and she sets aside more time for "quality leisure". She vows not to watch television in the evenings, reads more books, and goes out more often with her boyfriend. The impression I get is that she is willing for me to guide her and I am struck by the degree to which she still feels the need for an authority to tell her what to do. A background fantasy that I entertain at this point is that Klara is uncon-sciously using me as a passport to adult life. She still appears very uncertain about whether she can "hold her own", and in me she obvi-ously finds someone who represents, to some extent, both her parents and her boyfriend. In the protected space of therapy, she can take a closer look at what they actually stand for. At the same time, I am certainly also a mirror that reflects and responds to the way she is.

After five sessions, we start homing in on Klara's autonomy and dependence problem. She imagines returning to the bosom of the family, where everything would be as it used to be: "But there's no room for me, my sister's boyfriend has moved in with her." I say to Klara, "If you were to really give in to your longing to return home, you would probably lose much of your courage and independence." She chimes in, "Especially as things weren't always so rosy there. But wanting to go back puts gilt on everything . . ." Subsequently, she recalls the constant bickering with her sister, from earliest childhood: "You always had to fight for your place." Without initially seeing any connection with this problem, Klara starts engaging with her jealousy. I am struck by the enthusiasm with which she describes her rivals, the way they move and dress, their provocative laughter. These idealised descriptions of her competitors culminate in fits of rage: "I hate them!"

After eight sessions, Klara tells me about a dream she has had:

> I'm playing a board game with my boyfriend. He is winning because I can't get on to the squares where his girlfriends' pieces are. On those pieces I see pictures of attractive brunettes. I just can't get on to these squares; he gets all the points and wins.

In connection with this dream, she realises that she cannot find a way back to herself if she is always looking at the others: "Then I can't find out what I really want and what I'm capable of." Subsequently, she talks about her own interests. She concludes that so far she has been unable to genuinely engage with her studies because she is "always looking right and left to see how the others manage." In so doing, she loses sight of herself, forfeits her marked sense of curiosity, and neglects her own interests.

In this phase of therapy, Klara is concerned with her prospects for the future. I encourage her to take her time and tell me about them in detail. She imagines best- and worst-case scenarios, and her fantasies about the future give her greater clarity, confidence, and guidance. The diffuse, debilitating pressure to perform gives way to a conscious, active readiness to do well. In our exchanges, the erotic subject matter remains present but is relegated to the background. However, I am repeatedly struck by the vivacity with which she describes the coquettish, vamp-like behaviour of her rivals. She calls herself a "naïve little woman", using the same words with which she characterises her mother. I suggest that by adopting the submissive "female" role played by her mother, she is attempting to be faithful to her mother's approach to life. Her answer: "Perhaps I am hiding behind a naïve and dependent role." She mentions how ambitious she once was about her sporting activities. She hints at a desire for erotic experiments but refuses to tell me any more than that. Once I have indicated that she should spend more time talking about the vital and courageous sides of her nature, her liveliness and attractiveness become more apparent. She is able to experience her vitality more consciously. I support her in this, pointing out how she repeatedly conceals her liveliness behind the over-adjusted, long-suffering side of her character.

Halfway through therapy, Klara's inner struggle between an active, self-confident attitude to life and submissive suffering flares up in connection with her jealousy problem. The constantly recurring detailed descriptions of the "smouldering" allure of her competitors make it increasingly clear how unimportant her boyfriend is in all this. Sometimes, it seems as if she is not in love with him, but with her rivals. When I point this out to her, she is astounded initially but soon she starts to think and immerses herself in her own sexual desires and longings, comparing them with those of her girlfriends. During this stage, Klara makes better contact with herself; her dealings with her boyfriend are both more imperious and demanding but also more affectionate.

Klara starts to engage with her own body. Maybe her intestinal complaint did more to dislocate her body-feeling and her self-awareness than she was initially inclined to admit. At present, she finds herself "quite pretty" but still rejects her female contours as too angular. She finds her bosom and her behind too small and her blond hair and blue eyes unattractive. She finds ample, brown-haired, and brown-eyed women better looking. She says admiringly, "Brunettes come across as more passionate, in fact—if you'll excuse the word—as hornier." As Klara thinks about her femininity, I have the impression that she has become kinder to herself. She is able to engage with the two very heterogeneous self-images—erotic vamp and timid mummy's darling—more freely and more playfully. She asks herself how a relationship can be both passionate and secure at the same time.

In the final stages of this brief course of therapy, Klara turns to the issue of growing older and what her future life should look like. She does not want to wait until she is forty to have children, but she has doubts about whether she can rely on her future husband: "Men have it easier in life. They become more attractive as they grow older and then they grab themselves younger women. Their own wives are not so interesting for them when they get older." I remind Klara that this is a pattern that she has experienced in her own family and assure her that it is by no means necessarily the case. She responds, "That's right, I've seen women get more self-assured in later life. But then I'd have to lead an entirely different kind of life than my mother." I say, "And that would mean inner separation . . ." Klara says, "Looks like it's unavoidable."

The final sessions are largely devoted to the separation problem; Klara is planning to marry her boyfriend. My impression is that Klara has made considerable progress in her personal development. At the end of the twenty-five-hour course of brief therapy, her anxieties have receded to such an extent that she can stoutly face up to the task of sorting out her private life and her professional activities. As she leaves, Klara expresses her gratitude and willingly accepts my offer to visit or call me and talk about the way things have shaped up one year hence.

After that year has elapsed, Klara contacts me full of beans. She has passed her exams and discovered that music is "a good companion." The only thing that worries her is the "power games" with her fiancé. "But I'm not the only one," she adds. Two years later, Klara calls me to ask for advice in connection with a job offer. We go through the pros and cons and at the end of our conversation she rings off cheerfully, saying "I'll get back to you if I need anything."

On that occasion, I ask her what good she thought the therapy had done her. She answers spontaneously, "I was going through a sticky patch. You were there for me to talk to; that gave me security. At the time, no one else gave me security and self-confidence." Klara was obviously in a threshold situation and was looking for a reliable, neutral companion. She goes on to say that it quite simply "did her good" to be able to talk about her problems: "Somehow, I felt understood." Initially, she had been apprehensive about confiding in a "complete stranger", but this fear had soon yielded to a feeling of having the freedom reveal everything. This had made many things easier and enhanced her awareness of them.

Klara welcomed the fact that I had offered her advice at the outset and had talked to her "quite normally". My "gentle pressure" not to avoid situations she was afraid of was another thing she had found helpful. On the other hand, she felt it to be important that I had later given her the requisite degree of latitude when it came to her unconscious relational conflicts. Before therapy, she had been unaware of how deeply she was immured in conventional man–woman stereotypes: "I would never have imagined that, like so many women and men, I might be afraid of independence and sexual confidence."

In my view, the reason why Klara had been able to relinquish her inappropriate behaviour, rid herself of unrealistic convictions, and work on unconscious conflicts was that she used the therapeutic relationship as a sounding board. This gave her a chance to mobilise her creative resources. As with the other patients, we see here different elements at work, taking over from one another in different stages of treatment. A reliable and supportive therapeutic relationship (A); behaviour orientated interventions militating against avoidance strategies and leading to more self-efficacy (B); discussing opinions and attitudes that distort reality, thus leading to better-defined attitudes (C); insight into unconscious conflicts making relational problems easier to understand (D). With the aid of the therapeutic interviews, Klara ultimately learnt to make better use of her creative resources (E). These factors will become more visible as we work our way through the other cases.

Two years after our last meeting, I received a phone call from Klara's mother informing me that Klara had been involved in a road accident and suffered a complicated fracture of the pelvis. She was to be operated on the next day. Klara was beside herself with anxiety and despair and she badly needed my assistance.

I visited Klara in hospital and she really did seem to be frightened and desperate. "I was doing so well," she said, "and now this!" She is afraid she will not wake up from the anaesthetic and will not be able to realise all her plans. We talk for a while, which reassures her somewhat. Some of her optimism returns. After the operation she wants to find out why she is so quick to think that this is the end of everything, and asks if we could arrange for a few more therapy sessions.

In the first few weeks after the operation, it is important to focus on stabilising and supportive aspects. On the behavioural level, we still need to fight against her avoidance tendencies. When she is physically restored, she says she will do her best not to have to face other people because she feels "somehow damaged". There is nothing we can achieve at the cognitive level. We discuss at great length just how irrational her attitude is, but Klara still finds it impossible to rid herself of this feeling of being damaged and, hence, inferior. For this reason, she wants to embark on a lengthier stretch of therapy so that on the couch she can investigate the ideas that occur to her.

Reclining on the couch twice a week, Klara does indeed manage to get in contact with important memories. As she asks herself why she is so jealous of brown-haired, dark-eyed women, she utters the word "hate". Strictly speaking, such feelings should be taboo: "Isn't it terrible? There I am looking after my patients as best I can, trying to be a good person, and all of a sudden I'm overwhelmed by feelings of hatred. It just can't be."

In a laborious process of self-examination, Klara manages to unearth feelings and fantasies that she has long since rejected and repressed. She comes up with a number of insights. She experienced her physical illness at the age of eighteen as annihilating. Everything she had been good at was suddenly beyond her. She was poor in class and unremarkable in sport. The worst thing was that her parents no longer regarded her as their "little ray of sunshine". In a long course of psychotherapy, she ultimately realised that her despair had been so crippling because an old wound had been reopened.

First, this wound came in the guise of a harmless memory. When she was three, her little sister was born and she no longer wanted to go to nursery school. Ultimately, however, she was forced to attend kindergarten. During psychoanalysis, Klara senses how intense her feelings were at the time. "They wanted me out of the house, someone else had taken my place." Initially, Klara refuses to acknowledge that, at the time, she also entertained feelings of rage. However, she is aware of how little it takes to make her feel belittled and forsaken, responding with "impotent rage that ruins everything". She finds it increasingly plausible that her childhood experiences, reactivated by her physical illness, make her respond to conflicts with self-damaging rage.

As of her third year, and in response to exclusion and her own rage, Klara developed into a well-adjusted little girl. She did everything her parents expected of her and turned into a good scholar. The best way of earning her father's affection was to follow in his footsteps and become good at tennis. Even after puberty she remained well behaved and disciplined. She considers this to be the foundation for her professional success and cultural interests. The drawback is that she lives in constant latent fear that if she developed wishes of her own and stopped being such an achiever, the others would no longer love her and would immediately abandon her. That is why even the most piffling disagreements with her husband are so dangerous. They reactivate a "very old" feeling of abandonment that she quickly responds to with anger and despair without even realising it.

It took a long course of therapy for Klara to find out just how deeply rooted her anxieties were. In one session, she is alarmed at my referring to her feelings of hatred and anger: "No, it's impossible, I never have feelings like that." Then she drifts into a kind of trance in which she imagines the despair she felt as a little girl when she was "pushed off" to kindergarten. She says she can physically feel the pain she felt when she had the feeling of being "outcast". She had a similar feeling at eighteen, when the doctors had despaired of curing her and "gave her up". I ask her whether rage, or even hatred, might not be an understandable reaction in such a case. She thinks about this and starts engaging with unpleasant feelings that she rejects: "I don't want to be like that." I tell her that this is a way of splitting off important feelings and thoughts. "Yes," she says, "deep down I still want to be a good girl and not cause my parents any worries."

Klara senses that the price for a perfect façade is the suppression of important feelings: "They're lurking somewhere deep down inside me and only reveal themselves as ill-defined bad moods that I have no explanation for." Now she understands why even the slightest suspicion of being "dissed" by her husband makes her react so sensitively. She immediately feels pushed aside, which fills her with impotent rage. This is also the foundation for her jealousy. As if she were a figure in some psychotherapeutic manual, she remembers that when her sister was born, she had brown hair and was later admired by her own friends for her dark eyes.

Once Klara has re-experienced the feelings and fantasies that she has been repressing, she is also better able to react appropriately and with greater awareness to professional criticism. While we were working on her memories and dreams, we never lost sight of the situation she was in at a given moment. The following narratives will show how these different dimensions intermesh.

Klara asked to be given the story of her therapy to read. She requested some minor modifications to ensure her anonymity. Her comments closed as follows: "This is probably the way it was. But it's not so easy to find yourself portrayed so realistically."

Social anxiety: a business management student fails whenever things come to a head

"I feel best playing computer games. They shut out the whole world"

J oachim is a twenty-five-year-old business management student. He has just failed his oral exams. He felt "completely blocked" and could not answer even the simplest questions. The professor examining him is astonished to see his student go to pieces in this way. Joachim has always been an excellent student: his first-part finals earned him an A grade, "as everyone had expected". After the disastrous orals, he reluctantly allows his professor to make an appointment for him with me.

At our first encounter, Joachim is reserved and suspicious. He is very tall and slender and makes a troubled, unsettled impression. Avoiding eye contact with me, he reports stumblingly on the exam he has just failed: "There's no future left for me, having to go to a shrink is as bad as it gets. If they try to put me in a psychiatric ward, I'll jump out of the window first." He appears badly scared, his hands are shaking and he can hardly sit still. "I just don't know what's wrong with me," he says.

Asked about his earlier life, Joachim says that achievement has always been the most important thing. He has always wanted to perform some extraordinary feat. As far back as he can remember, he has intended to follow in his father's footsteps. From his first day in school, he was determined to become a professor—like his father. In school, he was top of the class but never had any real friends. He gave physical games and sporting activities a wide berth. This is reflected in his appearance. His posture is bowed, his movements hectic; he hardly seems to inhabit his own body. His favourite leisure-time activities underline this distance from his bodily self. He enjoys playing computer games and watching science fiction films. "Then the whole world is shut out," he says. Although he plays an active role in a student initiative of a social nature, he has no close friends. He has never had a girlfriend: "That saves a lot of friction."

At the end of our first interview, I recommend a number of attitudes and behaviours designed to help him pass the exam the second time round. In so doing, I stick to three rules I have described in my book on creativity between creation and destruction (2011): accept problems and setbacks, devise productive rituals, use the scope at your disposal. More explicitly, I suggest that Joachim should simply acknowledge the fact that, for once, this exam was something that did not run perfectly. Second, we debate whether going for a run once a day might help him to relax. He thinks that working in the library at certain predetermined times could be a good idea. Third, I put it to him that in the evening it would be better for him to go for a walk, listen to music, or read a book than spend part of the night surfing the internet. When it comes to deciding what to do with his leisure time, it might also be a good idea in the present crisis to stop avoiding any kind of personal contact. For example, we discuss whether it might not be good for him to overcome his disinclinations and have lunch with his fellow students. At the end of our session, he surprises me by showing a degree of trust despite his initial suspicions. He agrees for us to meet a second time and says, "Maybe it is a good idea to talk."

We begin the second interview with Joachim describing his anxieties and despondency a second time. Then I ask him whether he has found any of my suggestions useful. He answers by saying that basically he could have hit upon those changes of behaviour himself. "But when you're in a crisis, you can't see the wood for the trees," he says.

It had done him good to trot round the nearby running track once or twice in the mornings. He has taken to going to the library to learn for the exam and ending his work at a specific time. The hardest thing for him is to give up his computer games and "rub shoulders" with his fellow students. We spend some time discussing how he can fight his avoidance behaviour and improve his work and leisure-time rituals.

At our third meeting, Joachim tells me about his efforts to "get his feet back on the ground" with the help of the behaviours we had talked about. He regularly goes for a run, he is able to prepare for his exam in the library, and he has an occasional coffee with his fellow students. Urged on by me, he has, after a long interval, attended one of the meetings of his social initiative group. It had not been easy; some of the members were alarmed at the way he looked and had asked him why he was in such a bad way. However, it was still good "to get out of the house". Towards the end of this supportive exchange, he expressed his hope that he would be able to get back out of the "hole" he was in. Although he does not really believe that I am interested in "what he gets up to", he is slightly more fluent in his accounts of his activities. On brief occasions, he reminds me of a child happy to be able to burble on to someone.

After two more sessions, Joachim tells me that he now goes for a half-hour run every morning. He finds this calming and has started actually looking forward to it. He also feels somewhat stronger. He has re-embarked on his exam preparations "with gusto". He has acted upon my recommendation to sort himself out in connection with his work routines, finishes the day's work at the same time, and subsequently rewards himself with a long walk. He says that his anxieties have receded into the background somewhat. Indirectly, he gives me to understand that our sessions have become important for him. He still jokes about "shrinks", but is grateful for the offer to prolong our meetings. It apparently does him good to have a reliable resource with whom he can discuss his problems.

Alongside our discussion of more general topics, we also prepare for the next exam. Along the lines of the stimulus exposure approach used in behavioural therapy, we imagine the exam situation in detail: time and place, the reactions of the examiners, his own feelings and expectations. After another session, Joachim reports that he has passed the exam with a B+ grade. Although this result is "not ideal", he is "fairly satisfied". We now begin to engage with his expectations at an intellectual level.

At the seventh session, Joachim tells me that he has passed another exam. He has also been meeting up with his friends. In our exchanges, however, he still makes an anxious, excitable, unstable impression. In a hunched-up posture, his eyes staring, he tells me that there is a girl student he would like to get to know better, but he is too shy. I invite him to imagine an encounter with the girl and give a graphic account of it, but he immediately shies away from the thought. He has never kissed a girl and his body feels like a "strange being" to him. This complete rejection of physicality communicates itself in his outward appearance and it worries me. On the other hand, he has come much closer. He draws his chair up very close as if to soak up my bodily aura. From this, I conclude that he has an ambivalent desire to get nearer to himself and to others. I do not feel it would be a good idea to put this to him, but I do resolve to keep an eye on this longing for physical proximity. At the end of the session, Joachim tells me that his acute crisis is more or less over but he would like another meeting to discuss where to go from here.

At the next session, Joachim appears more vital. The image I have is that of a fresh, intelligent boy who greatly looks forward to our encounters. As usual, he gives me a blow-by-blow account of his student activities. Now his exams are over, he has found an interesting research group and is already "half way through" his diploma thesis. Then he starts talking about his computer games and the contact between us dissolves. Yet, at the same time, I sense his longing for greater closeness. Accordingly, I ask him about the girl student he had his eye on. "I can't imagine what it's like to touch another person," he says.

His own body is alien to him. The mechanistic way he talks about his body and his feelings actually makes me shudder. I invite him to imagine out loud what tender contact with a girlfriend might be like. Spontaneously, he remembers a dream:

> I'm sitting in a train travelling through a half-destroyed city. I am the adjutant of the supreme commander who has ordered the destruction of the city.

Jokingly, Joachim asks whether there is an instruction kit or computer programme I could use to analyse the dream. I tell him that every dream has a subjective meaning. He responds by saying that he is unaware of anything destructive in his character: "I never break anything." I ask him whether he really never has destructive desires. His spontaneous answer is: "Then I just turn myself off." "Is that possible?" He goes on to say that he prefers to be constructive, but then he remembers something. "When I was a boy I used to hurl my toy cars at the window when I was in a temper."

He still gets impatient very quickly when something goes wrong. "Maybe that's why I avoid talking to girls," he says. "I couldn't stand being given the brush-off." In that respect, his sister is very different. She is calmer, more systematic, takes a long-term view of things. His mother says that was because of the pregnancies. In his sister's case, she was much more equable and relaxed. She had much more stress when she was expecting Joachim. His father had been given a professorship abroad, and the family lived in a socially disadvantaged part of the city. His mother felt constantly threatened and their flat was burgled on various occasions: "We had a very difficult time." His mother thinks that was probably why he was born early and had to spend several weeks in an incubator. With an odd kind of pride, he remarks that that was probably when he learnt to "dissociate himself from bodily things".

His parents told him that, as a child, he was sensitive and quickly annoyed. I suggest that being sensitive can have its advantages. Early on in life, he learned to respond to his environment with vigilant intelligence. Intellectually, he was very adept at finding his way in the world but maybe he did not feel really at home in his own body and had developed a degree of physical detachment as a form of self-protection. Joachim's response to this interpretation is reflective. He leans back in his chair and, for the first time in my presence, closes his eyes as if he were listening down inside himself.

In fifteen further sessions, Joachim immerses himself in the history of his family. His grandfather was a successful university professor. For his parents, professional status also played a dominant role, as did self-discipline. Although they identified outwardly with the student uprising of the late 1960s, deep down they remained highly traditional and achievement orientated. Status and success were their guiding values. Joachim recalls his parents' fear of infection. Physical contact was avoided. He, too, has become a "hygiene fanatic", he says. For all that, his upbringing was "really quite loving". In the last analysis, his parents enabled him to make something of himself, both vocationally and personally. The only thing he had to do without was social contact with children his own age: "That I really missed!" Despite his liberal upbringing, he thinks of sex as something dirty. "Masturbation is absolutely disgusting, I'd never do that!" I am amazed to come across such an attitude in the present day and age.

I find the way he talks about women actively alarming: "So far I've not had my sights on one that was worth firing at." However, in the further course of our exchanges he does embark on less antagonistic fantasies. Gradually, he starts to understand why he finds contact with girls so dangerous. At school and university, his social anxieties and puny stature meant that no girl would "touch him with a bargepole". Accordingly, he imagined what was unattainable to be unworthy of attainment. He thought of more virile and attractive young men and the girls they went out with as "animals". In short, he disparaged what he yearned for. At the same time, he started believing that there must be something fundamentally wrong with him. He even goes so far as to call himself "unworthy of living", immediately conceding that (because of its Nazi connotations) the phrase was in very poor taste.

At this stage of his treatment, his own life–work balance plays only a marginal role. Joachim seems more stable and is willing to engage with the past. His father and grandfather are idealised figures high above him. He is reluctant to think about their more difficult and unpleasant sides. He apparently fears that his ideals might start crumbling and that he would then be unable to get his feet back on the ground. Yet, ultimately, he does manage to draw a more realistic picture of these powerful personalities and to find a way back to his own self. Finally, day and night dreams dominate the sessions. As he begins to get to grips with his own yearnings, he meets a young woman who is obviously very fond of him.

After twenty-five sessions, Joachim wants to terminate his treatment. I believe that a more far-reaching course of psychotherapy would be preferable, but Joachim insists that now he can "carry on alone". In his summing up at our last meeting, he asserts that he has got the better of his anxieties and that he can continue with our exchanges as a kind of internal dialogue: "Don't worry about me!" But I am worried and try in vain to persuade Joachim to reconsider his decision. Sometimes, life itself heals the old wounds.

Two years after completion of therapy, Joachim sends me an "interim report" by email. Joachim's assessment of his treatment is that "it put me back together so that now everything's in working order again". In the context of an academic project, he has met a young woman, Sybille. There are parallels here to his relationship with Monika, the girl who turned up towards the end of his therapy. He says that maybe he is better at this kind of thing after the "crash course in establishing relationships" he went through with Monika. He can imagine getting married to Sybille: "Then there'll be this exciting race between me and my sister. Which of us will finally come up with little grandchildren for our parents?"

Three years later, Joachim sends another email saying that careerwise things are working out better for him all the time. He traces this back to our therapeutic exchanges. Sometimes, he still feels like a "nerd" but both he and the others can live with that. Recently, he had had "a strange, interestingly morbid dream". It reminded him of me and he said he was glad that he could make use of his dreams and fantasies to understand his situation better. For all that, "some of the skeletons in my psychic cupboard" still cause him trouble. He is separated from Sybille; they were living too far apart and they both felt the decision was sensible. His new girlfriend, of six months' standing, is Christine. "Neither of us are getting any younger and we both want children." He wants to make sure that "nothing will go wrong this time."

Six months later, I receive a wedding announcement, another year later an email with a letter of gratitude. The photo in the attachment is of Joachim with his little son on his lap. His wife has found an interesting research job. This has prompted him to discontinue his academic career, learning from his little boy "quite different sides of life".

Planning to write this book, I ask him via email whether the course of therapy, now seven years past, had helped him and, if so, how. His answer arrives the same day: "Absolutely. Your presence helped me to talk." Gradually, he had lost his inhibitions: "You know how sceptical I was about psychotherapy." Then there were the behaviour rules: regular physical exercise, well-defined work and leisure rituals. "I started to understand my own story and accept my body. You gave me courage. Thank you."

With reference to the psychotherapeutic ABCDE model, which I explain to him briefly, I ask him to say which dimensions of the model were important in his case. In his reply, he says that, initially, the stabilising and actively supportive elements were most important. My attention and sympathy had made him more confident. I ask him to assess the quality of the therapeutic relationship on a scale from 0 (completely negligible) to 10 (maximum significance). He gives the therapeutic relationship nine points, the role of behaviour-orientated interventions (B) eight. Intellectual reflection about negative attitudes (C) receives six points. He also considers insight into biographically induced conflicts and engagement with fantasies and dreams (D) important, giving this a score of eight. The therapeutic exchanges had encouraged him to accept his feelings, thoughts, and social experiences as something to be worked on. This aspect (E) gets full marks (ten).

Anxiety and avoidance: a pianist is afraid to demonstrate her prowess

"Things are going downhill fast"

Maria (twenty-eight) comes to me for psychotherapeutic treatment because, in the past few months, the "subliminal anxieties" that have dogged her for years have got worse. She says she has always had difficulty making new acquaintances. Slight changes in her environment make her feel helpless. She would like nothing more than "to show what I'm capable of" but she now believes that there is something pathological about her nervousness, which is compounded with palpitations, trembling, and sweaty palms. At school, she would invariably blush when the teacher asked her a question. For many years, she has also been subject to a fear of being alone. Driving a car gets her "uptight"; she avoids air travel. In the past few months, things have got "really bad". Various doctors have "not found anything" and prescribed tranquillisers, but this cannot be a long-term solution. She is getting more timid all the time; sometimes she feels "really desperate". She is afraid of becoming dependent on the tablets. In the past few years, she has also been the victim of frequent infections, rashes, and back pains. Things are "going downhill fast".

Asked about her present situation, Maria tells me that she has just embarked successfully on a career as a pianist. Her anxieties are, however, a major handicap. Her fear of flying is particularly serious: "In my profession it's an absolute no-go." She believes her anxieties have to do with leaving home. She frequently wakes up from nightmares in which her parents die of cancer, their house goes up in flames, or other terrible things happen. When her friend has to go away on business, she has visions of disaster, as if everything were over.

Maria describes her childhood as "wonderful". Her eyes light up as she tells me about her loving mother, her dependable father, and the big garden. However, after a few sessions, "very different things" start occurring to her. She recalls that in the case of her younger sister, her mother's pregnancy was very complicated. Her mother was frequently ailing, was periodically restricted to her bed, and had little time for her. She herself cannot remember this period but her father has told her about it. After the birth, her mother concentrated her attentions on her sister. She was slightly retarded in her development and everyone was worried about her. Maria recounts her first memory: "My little sister is throwing my toys around and breaking everything." At the time, she felt helpless to do anything about this but she cannot recall anger or resentment. When another sister was born three years later, "I pounced on her and wouldn't let anyone else look after her." She remembers that, at the age of six, she was proud of "already being like my mother".

Maria describes her puberty as unremarkable: "I was always well-adjusted and easy to handle." The trouble started when she noticed the physical changes taking place. Even today she regards her breasts and her other female features as alien: "I'd really prefer to be a child." She was good at school, which gave her mother much pleasure. Her musical gifts became apparent early on and prompted her to study the piano. However, when she performs in public, she has the feeling of floating in a vacuum and losing all contact with the ground. This frequently makes her think of her mother, a very successful physician, sometimes exaggeratedly devoted to her profession. She often fears that her mother disregards her own interests to such an extent that she is "completely drained". He father is quite different. He is a lawyer, takes things more comfortably, never wears himself down to the bone. He has a good grip on life and looks after the family matters that have to do with the outside world.

Maria comes across as very likeable. She has cheerful, shining blue eyes, is charming, and expresses herself very fluently. Only in the later encounters does she reveal a more timid, diffident, and despondent side. I then have the feeling that she is entering a realm of shadows that contrasts starkly with the bright side of her character. The impression I get is that of a nice, well-behaved girl whose main concern is to make herself pleasant to others. Yet, in this, she also comes across as slightly superficial. She appears to be apprehensive about the passionate sides of her nature. She experiences them as dark forces jeopardising her social adjustment. On the other hand, she asks herself, "What do I really want?"

Maria fills the first few sessions with descriptions of her anxieties. She recounts many nightmares in which her parents lose their lives. The second dominant subject is her fear of flying. One dream has recurred more than once:

> I'm hanging on the wing of an aeroplane, feel myself slipping off and can't hold on much longer.

She imagines a whole string of disasters. After a while, these subjects recede into the background as she starts to engage with her feelings of loneliness and abandonment. She is aware that a career in music will mean taking leave of many things, notably her parents and also her loveless relationship with the man in her life, a relationship that "basically has long since come to an end". However, she has not left him because if she did, she would feel alone and unattached. For her, independence is synonymous with abandonment and isolation.

The threshold situation in which she finds herself becomes more and more apparent. On the one hand, she has offers for concerts abroad; on the other, she is reluctant to do without the piano lessons she gives at home. This ambivalence is also a characteristic of her femininity. On the one hand, she wants to be the caring girl she has always been; on the other, she is keen for adulation. "What I'm afraid of is not the envy of my rivals but the fact that there may be no way back."

In this connection, she has a dream:

> I'm in complete despair because during a concert tour I've forgotten that my parents and my husband have died.

The dream shows her the conflict between her desires for autonomy and dependence. As she contemplates this, she appears lighter and more cheerful: "It does me good to look things in the face." Accordingly, Maria uses the first few sessions to talk about and contemplate the past and her present world. However, we also discuss practical everyday rituals that might enable her to come to terms with her anxieties. It helps her to imagine fraught situations in my presence and discover alternative behaviours. I also encourage her to take long walks, which have been beneficial in the past, and do relaxation exercises. My behaviour-orientated advice is in no way detrimental to our work on her unconscious wishes and conflicts. On the contrary, Maria feels more secure when I talk to her about her present worries and propose practical solutions.

During treatment, Maria's courage in perceiving repressed desires and unconscious urges increases. In our psychotherapeutic exchanges, she embarks on a "journey of her own" without constantly having to reassure herself that her friend and her parents and siblings are still there. It surprises her that this does nothing to weaken her relationships; in fact, it gives them greater depth. Her anxieties recede in the process. Central topics now are things like the tensions between maternity and a career: "If I want to be a concert pianist, how can I have children? And what about the right husband?" She sees a conflict between attachment and passion: "During sex I just go flying away, I feel completely free, but I don't know who I'm with." She believes sexual pleasure could jeopardise her relationship: "You always fly alone, don't you?" Towards the end of her treatment, she broaches the question of creative development: "How and where can I make the most of myself?"

After twenty-five sessions, Maria concludes that her anxieties have greatly improved. She can fly "with collywobbles in my stomach" and has accepted a number of engagements. She believes she has become more courageous. In the background, feelings of uncertainty still lurk, notably in connection with flying. She sees them as indications that "something is happening inside me". She says she is not really afraid of flying; she has fears of loss, which have probably dogged her all her life. She has a clearer view of her conflicts and is glad to be able to "play more freely with my desires, hopes, and fears".

In retrospect, Maria feels more unburdened as a result of being able to talk about herself and her anxieties. At an intellectual level, she used my advice to confront her anxieties. Engagement with flying and the fear-reducing rituals alleviated her fears but the essential thing was that she found a space in which to perceive repressed desires and engage with existential conflicts such as the rival claims of staying cosily at home and going out to conquer the world. Maria took a greater degree of confidence with her and, at the end of her brief course of therapy, made a more authentic and secure impression. Her professional career took her abroad and I told her I hoped she could make further creative use of the stimuli she had received. Two years later, she sent me a birth announcement with a nice photo of her first daughter: "I've changed course. I'm a teacher now, and as you can see, I'm very happy."

Ten years after completion of her therapy, I ask Maria's permission to publish extracts of her treatment record in an anonymous form. She consents to this and, during a long phone call, she says she still thinks back to our exchanges. Sometimes, she remembers individual sentences or insights. Her treatment is like an inner companion that she is fond of recalling. It helped her to find out what she really wanted. "Now I have achieved what I dreamt of for myself: one girl, two sons." She also enjoys her secure status as a teacher. Most of her colleagues are fond of grousing, but she enjoys her work. There were some problems after the birth of her first daughter. Her maternity and her husband's career stress made it difficult for them to live out the erotic side of their relationship: "It could have gone badly wrong." But then, after a few months and with the help of the grandparents, they managed to create some space for themselves and found their way back to one another. Today, they are good at dealing with the permanent tension between the claims of attachment and the passionate desire for freedom.

Asked what it was in psychotherapy that might have helped her, Maria refers to the opportunity of talking in a congenial atmosphere and being able to say whatever she liked. She awards ten points to the significance of the therapeutic relationship (A). Behaviour-related interventions (B) were also important and she gives them seven points. The intellectual correction of dysfunctional views and opinions (C) was of minor importance (two points). She finds it difficult to evaluate the engagement with unconscious conflicts, but finds it in no way insignificant. She awards this five points. Most important was the opportunity to talk and the possibility of being understood and responded to. She gives this existential dimension ten points, noting that she finds it all but impossible to distinguish it from the general significance of the therapeutic relationship (A).

Slight to moderate depression: a young woman doctor cannot explain why she feels so low

"It's as if I'm standing next to myself, and that's when I get scared"

In the past few weeks and months, Monika has been to see her family doctor on various occasions. He prescribes psychotherapy. She tells me that for years she has been suffering from an "odd kind of tension and anxiety". Sometimes, she feels really low and cannot say why: "It's as if I'm standing next to myself." She has never attached any great significance to all this, but this changed during the stressful preparations for her first medical degree examination, which brought about stomach troubles, irregular menstruation, and violent headaches. First she feared she might have abdominal cancer, later a brain tumour, or something like that. Both her family doctor and her gynaecologist did their best to reassure her, telling her that the symptoms were caused by stress. Various tranquillisers and homeopathic remedies proved ineffective. The antidepressive drug amitriptyline did calm her down a little, but she feels "as if I'm not there".

Her parents tried to help her. Her father took her on a journey to take her mind off things, but she had to break it off prematurely because of constant nausea and anxiety. Her earlier fears of public spaces, bridges, and high buildings became so severe that she withdrew from social life completely: "Today I reduce my social activities to an absolute minimum." She is increasingly afraid of her own anxiety, sometimes all she could think of was "fear, fear, fear". On the subject of her life so far, Monika tells me that she grew up in a "picture-book family". Things were more or less perfect, Monika was the youngster, her sister was five years older. Their mother was a mother "through and through". She gave up her career as a doctor for the sake of the children and was always a caring mother, if anything a little over-protective. Perhaps she was this way inclined because she was already fairly old when she had her daughter. Her father was also nearly fifty. Although he was a specialist, he always had enough time for his children, unlike many of his colleagues. During her childhood, the family moved around a lot, and on one occasion she was so exasperated at these removals that she tore up her nappies. She was late attending kindergarten because her mother was so anxious to look after her. That was when she started having severe nightmares. She frequently awoke from them in tears, asking herself, "What will it be like when my parents are no longer there?" She recalls that dreams like this still persisted when she was in primary school.

Monika describes her puberty as "unspectacular". There were never any conflicts or altercations with her parents. Even in puberty, she was still convinced that her father was the "ideal husband": "I hope I can find someone like that, not someone where you're afraid it'll all be over in three or four years." At twenty, her girlfriends noticed that she was the only one who still went on holiday with her parents. At sixteen she had fallen in love for the first time, but the relationship with her same-age boyfriend was "too unsettled" for her. She preferred hobnobbing with her sister's friends, who were much older. She considered them "more intellectually challenging and cultivated than the roughnecks in my class." However, she never entered into a close relationship with any of them and "there was never anything sexual about it." But today she does not feel that she missed out on anything.

In our therapeutic relationship, Monika initially makes a worldly-wise, self-confident impression. She broaches topics of general interest to demonstrate her intellectual assurance. Emotionally, things are very different. On this plane, the effect she has on me is one of apprehensive fragility concealed behind her over-ample figure. Sometimes, she reminds me of a very clever but also very insecure, indeed almost desperate, little girl.

Our first five sessions are taken up with Monika's descriptions of her ailments. She hardly dares leave the house, her head hurts, maybe there's "something there" after all? However, she does seem somewhat reassured by my calm attention, as if she were gaining security. She says it is a good thing that "you never get het up." Encouraged by the interest I evince, the focus in each session gradually changes to her activities: the quest for a topic for her dissertation, recent films, political issues. At first, she is astonished by my interest in her concerns, but, in terms of "self-efficacy" it also gives her the feeling that she can contribute something worthwhile to her own therapy. The intellectual exchanges she involves me in seem to give her greater security; sometimes, she gives me an impish grin when she thinks she has successfully diverted me from my psychotherapeutic interpretations.

Once she has established a trusting relationship, we go to work on a training programme. I advise her to go for walks at predetermined times because in the past she found such walks relaxing and they helped her get her ideas sorted out. She finds it plausible that this might also be a way of getting to grips with the physical concomitants of her anxiety. My second suggestion is that she should gradually start revisiting the places she is afraid of. Third, in the form of a Socratic dialogue, we discuss the irrational nature of her anxieties.

During the first few sessions, Monika repeatedly asks whether her anxieties might not go away altogether if she took more tablets or tried hypnosis. Finally, I put it to her that her anxieties might have a meaning. Her answer is that looking for the significance of her anxieties would be like trying to examine the fangs of a ravening wolf about to pounce on her. I remark that this wolf might be of interest for her. Her response is, "Do you think that it would then change into an affectionate dog." "Why not?" I ask, and Monika remembers her own dog, a trusty companion in her childhood.

At this point we begin to play with images that I consider to be symbolic representations of her diffuse anxieties. Here, the creative, psychodynamic stage of treatment starts gaining cogency. Monika delves down into her fantasies about animals that are aggressive but interesting, or affectionate but boring. She asks herself what this has to do with herself and her desires. Then she plucks up courage and engages with the question of potential partners. In the process she recalls alarming situations from her childhood. On one occasion, a swimming teacher espousing radically new methods of instruction held her head under the water for quite a long time. The result was "shattering"; she still cannot swim. She is surprised to find that talking about such memories and her reactions does not upset her but gives her the feeling of being more in accord with her own self.

As Monika engages with her fantasies, memories, and wishes, her present anxieties and physical ailments recede into the background. My impression is that she is gradually "forgetting" her symptoms. Yet, the full extent of her avoidance behaviour also becomes clearer. For years she has done without any emotionally involving attachments outside her primary family, and she also avoids completing her studies and looking for a job. These topics take centre stage eight weeks into therapy, when Monika is working on her autonomy–dependence conflicts. She dreams:

> I'm travelling in a train with my father and feel just fine. Suddenly, my father's no longer there, and I ask myself whether he's died. And then a driverless locomotive goes hurtling off into nothingness at breakneck speed.

Monika finds this dream "fairly interesting" but then makes fun of me when I tentatively suggest that the dream might have a meaning for her. In my eyes, it is a creative amalgamation graphically pointing up her desires for attachment and her separation anxieties.

After eight weeks (one session a week), Monika reduces her antidepressive medication of her own accord. But she still refuses to have any truck with my interpretations, one of them suggesting that she is afraid of autonomy and her own abilities because that would loosen the ties between her parents and herself. Triumphantly, she rejects my cautious conjectures: "I've been living on my own for years!" She tells me how audacious she had been when she travelled all through Italy with two girlfriends. She describes her flirtations with Italians like a nine-year-old girl with no hint of serious sexuality. The image she communicates to me is of one who is "above all sexual desires". But she offers me sexual topics, only to laugh at the ideas I come up with: "Well, what do you think? Psychotherapists probably always have their mind on sex anyway." My impression is that she wants to leave sexual topics to me so that she does not have to deal with them herself.

Monika recounts a dream she has had:

I'm at home with my parents and they give me a sweet little puppy for Christmas. I play around with it until I realise that it's getting bigger and finally it turns into a male fox. I transform myself into a snail leaving a trail of slime behind it. The fox catches my scent and sets off in pursuit of me.

Monika finds this dream repulsive and revolting, but she suspects that it might contain an important message. "I don't know what it is," she says, "maybe I don't want to know." I encourage her to stay with the dream and play around with it. First, she engages with the image of the puppy. At first it is sweet and playful, then it becomes a sexual being pursuing her. She remembers that in German "snail" is a vulgarism for the female genitals. Is this a dream of transformation, as in the fairy-tale where the frog changes into a prince? She feels she is more like Sleeping Beauty, the princess protected by a hedge of thorns. She imagines what it might be like if a man had designs on her, and for the first time asks herself what it means to be a woman. She says that she only knows herself as a nine-year-old girl and that is maybe how she wants to stay: "innocent, odourless, protected."

In this period, in which Monika, stimulated and encouraged by my responses, plays creatively with fantasies and dreams, her outside life also takes a turn for the better. She has found a supervisor interested in the subject of her dissertation. She is focusing her attention on the thesis and actively enjoying the process. There is hardly any more talk of symptoms. After another eight weeks—this is session sixteen—Monika talks about her sister's baby, which she refers to throughout as "the monster". Initially rather hesitant to use such drastic expressions, she finds herself encouraged by my attitude to come clean and say precisely what she feels and thinks: "The monster screams all day and is insatiable in its greed." For Monika, the monster baby becomes a creative metaphor. I suggest that it is perhaps necessary to accept the vitality of the monster baby. Monika says how important it has become for her to say what she thinks in our sessions even if it is "inappropriate". It enables her to engage with her own greed. She returns to the puppy and snail dream and thinks out loud about her sexual desires: "Am I putting myself at someone's mercy? Would I be loved or exploited? Can I get a man to stay with me?" She imagines what it would be like to give birth to a "monster baby".

Once the complaints that prompted her to seek therapy have abated, Monika starts thinking about the end of treatment. She has the following dream:

> My father has died. But he keeps on coming back, appearing to my mother and me and saying: "Want me to show you how to die?" Then he dies again, only to come back, over and over again . . . We tell him to stop doing that and stay away for good.

Monika prefers not to think about this dream and hopes I will not embark on any "wild psychoanalytic speculations". To me, the dream appears to be a creative narrative accompanying her psychic development, its imagery a condensation of her conflicts. I resolve to make an indirect allusion to the (for me) evident connection between valediction, death, and sexuality in the dream by enlarging on some of my ideas about Mozart's opera, *Don Giovanni*. Monika herself has told me about this opera, in which a father figure, the *Commendatore*, is killed by Don Giovanni. He returns as the "man of stone" and punishes Don Giovanni for his sexual profligacy by consigning him to Hell. I ask Monika about her own associations in connection with greed, sexuality, and death. Triumphantly, she says, "When I first had that dream, I was three years old!" This is her proof that the dream can have nothing to do with sexuality. I cannot refrain from asking her where she was sleeping at the time. She says she first had a cot in her parents' bedroom and then after that slept in their bed with them for quite a long time. Should I tell Monika about the significance of the primal scene, the observation of the parents engaged in the sex act? I decide not to, because here again the dream appears to me to be a metaphorical commentary on her present development. For the first time, she has met a young man and fallen in love with him.

In the final sessions, Monika returns to her animal metaphors. "Actually, it's a pity to make a pet out of such a wild animal," she says. Her attitude to the "monster baby" becomes more lenient: "Astonishing how much strength and vitality there is in such a small baby!" My enquiry about whether a prolongation of the brief therapy limited to twenty-five sessions might not be a good idea figures—among many other issues—in her last dream:

> I'm at home. The doctor there says I have a serious illness, leukaemia. The doctor here in Heidelberg says it's not true.

At the end of our time together, we sum up and ask ourselves what Monika has "got out of" her therapy.

Five aspects are central. The therapeutic relationship (A): Monika says it has done her good "just to talk". It was difficult at the beginning but she has realised that putting chaos into words is a good thing. It has also given her more courage to approach others.

Behaviour modification (B): the everyday routines have been a help. She intends to persevere with the regular physical exercises because they make her more mindful. She feels more stable when she is physically active and promises to force herself to engage in such activity when she feels "there's a crisis round the corner".

Correction of dysfunctional opinions (C): "I suppose my ideas about what I should be like were pretty rigid." She felt, however, that in future she did not need therapy to help her reflect on her attitudes and values.

Dynamics of unconscious conflicts (D): initially, working on unconscious conflicts had been "very strange". She had major doubts about whether immersing oneself in "all that slime and gunge" would do any good: "But now I actually enjoy talking things over when I've had an odd dream." She intends to draw upon fantasies and dreams in future and see them as commentaries on her life.

Understanding and communication as a creative task (E): Monika sees it as an entirely practical task to be more courageous in future about taking advantage of her own potential and more vigilant in trying to understand herself and others. The dialogue with oneself that takes place in dreams and fantasies is an "elixir". She also intends to make more active use of the inspiration she finds in books and films to make better sense of her own feelings.

One year after the end of treatment, Monika calls me on the phone because she intends to look for a different kind of job. We conduct three coaching exchanges on the phone during which Monika weighs up the pros and cons of her decisions. "At the moment" she has no psychic complaints. After another five years, I send Monika an email asking her for an interview looking back on her therapy. One day later, she tells me she would be happy to take part in a follow-up interview. We agree to talk on the phone because she lives a long way away. First, I ask her whether the treatment had done her any good. "Definitely," she replies. "Otherwise I'd still be in therapy and swallowing pills. I feel great and I'm really doing well in my job." She tells me that she has a managerial post in a large company and earns more than she can spend. She makes a cheerful impression and tells me that her private life is also very satisfactory. She enjoys life and has time for her cultural interests.

I ask her once again to look back and say what was most helpful about her therapy. Her spontaneous answer: "I could speak my mind." For this aspect (A), she awards ten points. "Then you always told me I should face up to situations I was anxious about. At first your insistence on physical exercise got on my nerves, I was always more like Churchill: no sports! But then your obstinacy about combating my avoidance behaviour did me good." So, eight points for (B). "I had plenty of time to scrutinise my ideas about myself and my relations with the world outside." She gives six points to the significance of these cognitive aspects (C). "Engaging with my past, the fantasies and dreams and their interpretations opened up new perspectives for me." Accordingly, the psychodynamic dimension (D) merits eight points. "The most important thing was, I felt well looked-after on the road back to myself. It made me more courageous and more open. I saw that reality is what I make of it." Monika gives a score of ten to the existential dimension (D).

Psychosomatic symptoms:
a housewife in pain for decades

"My husband puts me in the shade"

A sixty-five-year-old woman (I shall call her Hilde) calls me and asks for an appointment to discuss "marital troubles". She has always done everything for her husband, but he has had a girlfriend for years: "There's nothing I can do about it." In addition to the distress she has on this score, she complains of a variety of physical ailments and lives "in constant fear of cancer". She goes to the doctor's almost every day. "Everything hurts. If it's not my back, it's my head." At our first interview, it strikes me that she talks exclusively about her husband's life. She tells me how successful he is at his job, enumerates his preferences and inclinations. I ask her questions about her own life, but she ignores them as if they were not worth talking about. "My husband puts me in the shade," she says, her tone implying that this is what she deserves.

At our second session, she continues in this vein; I have no idea how to get in touch with her. This time she mentions not only her husband, but also a son. He has a chronic illness and "keeps her on her toes" although she never interferes in his affairs. Hilde's voice is monotonous and accusing. I feel rather bored and irritated. My attempts to bolster her self-confidence with appreciative remarks get me nowhere. I advise her to lead a more independent life, but my own counsels sound vacuous to me. The third session brings no change. Hilde is immaculately turned out and talks exclusively about her husband and her son's health issues. Again, I am assailed by feelings of boredom and futility. I trot out some "technical" recommendations about how to live in a relationship, but they sound flat and stale. To combat this emptiness, I let Hilde carry on talking and attempt to pay greater attention to my inner moods and images. After a while, I am actually rewarded by the emergence of a graphic scene played out in my mind's eye. I see a big stage on which Hilde's husband plays a variety of roles. He is not only the actor, he is also the director, occasionally he turns up in the auditorium, and he is in charge of the props. The son also makes a brief appearance. But where is my patient? I start to look for her. Is she back there in the shadows, in the recesses of the stage?

Finally, I tell Hilde about the image that has popped up in my mind: "You have come to me to raise the curtain on your inner stage. But the only figure to be seen is your husband with all his traits and quirks, his professional activities, and his connections. Sometimes I see your son as well, but I can't find you." Hilde pauses to think, starts talking about her husband again, realises the fact, and says, "I suppose you're right." I say, "Why don't we try and see where *you* are in all this." Hilde's answer comes automatically: "I'm not there. Probably I'm doing something backstage." I stick to the image. "Perhaps you're hiding behind the curtain of your duties?" I suggest. Immediately, I have a picture of a shy girl hiding in the shadows at the back of the stage. Hilde reflects for a moment and then says, "Something occurs to me. When I was a child, I wasn't so self-effacing, I took an interest in sex at quite an early age. There was a sixteen-year-old boy living opposite; he was awfully good-looking and had an electric guitar. I had a crush on him for a long time and finally plucked up the courage to talk to him. I took him home and proudly showed him my doll's house. He laughed his head off and left. I never dared to look at him again." Hilde tells this story as if it were a dream, and now I find it easier to relate to her feelings. She attempts to get back to the subject of her husband, but I insist that it is important for us to stay with her feelings and ideas.

She tells me how hard it has always been for her to be the focus of attention. Suddenly, as if in a dream, I see a lonely, despondent young woman. Accordingly, when she starts telling me mournfully and monotonously about her domestic duties and the trouble she has with plumbers and carpenters, I ask her once again to stay with her own story. Then she associates the scene of the young man who laughed her to scorn with a miscarriage she had at the beginning of her marriage. At the time, she felt very lonely and blamed her husband for avoiding the issue and hiding behind his work. But self-doubt is still there, lurking in the wings. "Perhaps I hide behind my husband because I don't trust my own feelings and thoughts," Hilde says. Once she goes off in search of her own wishes and fears, strengths and weaknesses, she seems more like her real self. I also feel closer to her.

At the outset, I had asked Hilde for an account of her life so far, but it had remained a mere collection of facts that I had hardly any memory of. Now that a creative therapeutic process had begun, I suddenly realised the significance of the "brother I always worshipped". At an early stage, Hilde learned to admire men and stay in the background. This gave her a close attachment to her mother, who behaved in the same way. Yet, at the same time, she sensed the more enterprising impulses within. She realises now that she used her docile and over-adjusted behaviour as a demonstration of loyalty to her mother. In this connection, Hilde tells me that her father also had a girlfriend for many years. She had never considered this important, but now she realises how she had to bite back her anger through all those years so as "not to smash any china". She finds it regrettable that this repression of "understandable feelings" also involved putting a damper on so much positive energy.

In the fifth session, Hilde tells me she has started attending a painting course so as not to spend the whole day looking for housework to do. At the next appointment, she proudly shows me a little watercolour she has done. She goes to the cinema with her friends and at the seventh session tells me about the film *Eyes Wide Shut*, an invitation to all kinds of sexual fantasies. She says no more about the film, but I recall the sex dreams acted out in the film and have the feeling that I am sifting through them on Hilde's behalf. Accordingly, I ask her whether the film aroused any emotional echoes I her. "Yes," she said guardedly, "but I don't want to think about them. What does the film mean to you?" I say, "You may be inhibiting the richness of your fantasies if you wait and see what your partner has to say." Hilde says, "I feel safer that way, though of course a lot of me does get lost in the process."

The eighth session merits a more detailed account. Before Hilde arrives, I resolve to ask her about her wishes and longings. The session before, she had said how difficult she found it to look them in the face. She opens the session by expressing her relief at the fact that the relationship with her husband has eased somewhat. She has no idea why. I assume that she has become more active and goes her own way more, which seems to have a beneficial effect on the relationship. As she then proceeds to talk about her everyday chores in house and garden and her visits to the doctor, I once again see in my mind's eye the stage, which Hilde is once again filling with props. I could tell her this, but instead I start enquiring more urgently after herself and her desires. I ask her about her dreams, because this is where wishes often find their clearest expression. She answers, "That's all just banal stuff." I say, "How so?" Hilde replies by recounting a dream:

> After visiting my brother I dreamt that he asked me if he could have my car. I said yes and then saw him driving at breakneck speed across a wide plain. Then the car takes off, flies through the air and lands with a big bang. My brother whoops with glee. The car is dented and I'm furious. I'm particularly angry because I have to repair the car.

Hilde adds that this anger has no place in their real brother-and-sister relationship, which is always "nice and friendly".

I think about the brother's vitality and about Hilde's more live-wire sides. What has happened to them? So, as she goes on lambasting this and other dreams as banal and nonsensical, I tell her that the car dream is very interesting. She says she has always got on well with her brother: "He was my hero and I was his favourite sister. My two little sisters had no significance for us. My brother had a great deal of influence on me and always put me on the right track." I say, "Perhaps he took too much off your shoulders and sometimes steam-rollered you a little with his activities?" Hilde: "Not really . . . though actually he can be very aggressive, even cruel. He had no qualms at all about telling my sisters to their faces that they looked 'absolutely idiotic'." She says that he often thinks of no one but himself and might, indeed, be called selfish. It was always quite clear that the one bicycle the children had belonged to him. He was often beaten for his impertinence and obstinacy. "Father only ever beat me once because I told a lie. I had pretended to be doing my homework but instead I was out on the streets with a girlfriend."

Hilde discards these topics for the rest of the session and returns to everyday matters. The image I have is of her leaving the stage and hiding behind the props. I say, "Perhaps you feel safer if you can hide behind your brother?" Hilde replies, "My husband has been much more attentive recently because I give vent a bit more to what I think." I say, "But there's still this tendency to leave the stage that stands for your life." Hilde: "I often talk to girlfriends who trace all their problems back to abusive fathers." I say, "What about your father?" Hilde says, "He was very affectionate . . . hmm . . . but also dreadfully authoritarian." I say, "Dreadfully?" I suddenly have a vision of her father's darker, unsettling side. Hilde muses, "Yes, it's odd. I always have this radiant memory of him—for example, I recall sitting on his lap in the car and it couldn't go fast enough for me. I was incredibly proud of father and his car. I cried when the car was sold. He secretly showed me photos from the war; he let me put on his peaked cap and his belt. Strange that I should find all that so marvellous." At this point, Hilde begins to engage with the darker sides of her father's past. He was not a Nazi, but he did not oppose them either. "We probably all have our lighter and darker sides," she says.

After this very general statement, she falls to thinking and for the first time in her life faces up to her father's involvement with National Socialism. It strikes me that during these investigations of the past she appears liberated rather than downcast. Hesitantly, she confronts the less admirable sides of her father's character. "Perhaps we women give our men such a glorious build-up because we can't stand their weaknesses," she says. During these reflections on her father's less laudable traits, she starts focusing on her mother as well.

"My mother ran the home. She was very good to me but also very serious. She couldn't play with us," Hilde says. The children were often too much for her mother, so Hilde did her best to be a good daughter. On one occasion, Hilde was top of the class at school. Her mother was proud but immediately admonished her not to give herself airs. Hilde herself finds her achievements unremarkable. I ask her why she always hides her light under a bushel. "Yes, I'm surprised how well I manage," she says. "Recently my girlfriends have actually

started listening to me. I can't think why, it's still the same old stuff."
It suddenly strikes me that Hilde looks more attractive now. Less
make-up, less hairspray, not as immaculately well dressed as before.
For the first time, she looks like someone you could reach out and
touch. Again, I ask her why she keeps putting herself down. Her
answer: "Perhaps since my childhood I've been afraid to stand out, to
show myself without make-up so as not to take any risks." I say, "The
price for that security is surely rather high if it means hiding your
wishes and abilities." Hilde says, "Yes, you've said that before. Maybe
there's something in it. My brother's such a power-pack . . ." I say,
"And yet it annoys you to let others have your car. Perhaps that's an
image for flexibility and vitality." Hilde: "Yes, but then they're the
ones to come a cropper." I say, "But you're the one who has to repair
the car." Hilde, with an ironical smile, "That's how the roles are
distributed."

After twenty-five sessions, Hilde is very much better. Her outlook
is positive, she has replaced her visits to the doctor with sporting and
cultural activities. I suggest prolonging therapy to get to grips with
more deep-seated conflicts. What I have in mind is her continuing
tendency to sell herself short. She keeps faith with her mother by iden-
tifying with her "subservient" attitude. This way, she can also uphold
an idealised image of her father, though she is fully and apprehen-
sively aware of the feet of clay it rests upon. Her fear of facing up
unflinchingly to her past and her future is still very obvious. In the last
few sessions I have also sensed the serious anger that has built up
behind her polite affability. Instead of risking open conflict with her
husband, she contents herself with "snide" remarks at his expense.
But when she turns down my offer to continue with psychotherapy, I,
too, feel devalued. "Thank you," she says. "I'm fine now."

Two years later, Hilde agrees to come for a follow-up interview.
She surprises me by saying that "by and large" she is fairly satisfied.
She can feel and accept herself more readily than she could before
therapy. "I've done a lot," she says. She has taken the therapeutic
exchanges as a stimulus to take a closer look at where she's coming
from and where she's going. "I've been getting to grips with the past,"
she says but does not enlarge on what precisely she means by that. I
am pleased to see that she's been exercising, dealing with her ortho-
paedic problems not only with conventional methods, but also with
Tai-Chi and regular swimming. She tells me her marriage has become

more respectful, and she has found a women's group where she can work out twice a week and also have a "heart-to-heart".

I give Hilde a brief run down on the ABCDE model and she awards her scores as follows: "Our conversations gave me strength and increased my self-confidence." In the individual categories she gives A, the general significance of a therapeutic relationship, eight points. About dimension B, she says, "You made me think about how I can modify my behaviour" and gives it six points. On category C, she says, "I was able to correct a number of negative attitudes" and gives this aspect four points. Then she goes on to talk about category D, the psychodynamic dimension: "At first I thought it was superfluous to talk about the biographical sources of my problems. But now it does me good to think about the possible causes of those conflicts." Category D receives seven points. Finally, Hilde evaluates the existential dimension (E), acceptance of life, as a job calling for creativity. "I've become more active and I cultivate my friendships," she says. "My marriage is more relaxed now. I see a number of things more playfully and I often think of those theatre and stage images of yours. That gives me more space to move in, I've got better at distinguishing important from unimportant and I have a better feeling for myself." Category E gets eight points.

Narcissistic personality traits: a law graduate sees no one but himself and despairs

"My mother and I: a wonderful couple!"

J ohann, a young law graduate, is "totally desperate" and no longer capable of systematic activity. He consults his family doctor because of tormenting moods, lack of drive, sleep disturbances, poor appetite, and weight reduction. His doctor sends him to me. His symptoms began after an additional course of study in England. He finds it important to emphasise that he was studying at an "elite university" and that he was the best graduate in his year. In England, he was offered an attractive research post, but he wanted to work in Germany. Before his return, he became increasingly insecure and started debating with himself what he should do professionally. Then it occurred to him that he would prefer to study music. He had played the cello at school and felt that as a musician one probably had more opportunities to "shine".

However, for weeks now, "hardly anything seems to be working." He takes no pleasure in his activities, feels listless, can no longer sleep, and sees no prospects for the future. The worst thing is his compulsion to "brood". "I'm just going round in circles," he says. It looks like a moderately serious depressive episode. Accordingly, I offer Johann psychotherapeutic sessions and recommend an antidepressive to help deal with his tormented self-interrogation and lack of drive. Only in the later course of therapy do I realise how serious his narcissistic conflicts are.

In the first sessions, Johann makes it clear that he feels accepted, supported, and well looked-after. It is obvious that my interest in what he has to say does him good. His shame at having to consult a "shrink" soon recedes into the background. Initially, he finds it banal of me to propose various ways of structuring his everyday life more effectively. We agree on regular meals, sporting activities, relaxation techniques. I also attempt to revive his interest in music. He attaches particular importance to my advice not to spend his evenings watching television or surfing the internet. "I had forgotten that it has always estranged me from myself," he says. I employ Socratic interview techniques to correct irrational convictions and depressive self-criticism, but with little success. He is convinced that he is a failure and that he will never be able to compensate for this "flaw" (his mental crisis).

After five sessions, Johann feels "just as bad as at the outset but, paradoxically, a little more optimistic." Perhaps "this business really is good for something." Music and running are helping him to find his way back to himself. Accordingly, I encourage him to carry on and set him "homework" to impose a rhythmic structure on the course of his day. Soon, a new topic starts dominating our exchanges. Johan tells me about his dreams of becoming a great musician. He listens to recordings of Pablo Casals and tells me of his ideas about becoming as popular and famous as the great cellist: "Just as long as I don't end up like my father: working all week and football on Saturdays." He likes playing for his father, although he senses that his "caterwauling" on the cello gets on his nerves, "But my mother admires me."

From early childhood, his mother has always accompanied him to his music lessons and class recitals. At secondary school, his fellow pupils made fun of him for that reason and, towards the end of his school career, he was the object of profound dislike, not to say enmity on the part of the other students. Although his grade average at graduation from school was 1.0 ("excellent") and he won a lot of prizes, this never made him arrogant (or so he says). But his schoolmates would have nothing to do with him and thought up tricks to play on him. Things were similar at his English university. He felt that he had always been helpful and showered compliments and gifts on the other students, "but they all found me arrogant and avoided contact with me."

In his quest for the reasons behind this treatment, Johann recalls a tendency he has to behave "like a queen". On one occasion he "got a little too physical" *vis-à-vis* a fellow student. But then the other suddenly withdrew, "I've no idea why." He still feels ashamed for approaching him in this way, especially as his friend then started "telling silly stories" behind his back. In our discussion of these topics, my therapeutic attitude is designed to take the pressure off my client. For example, I tell Johann that gifted people frequently arouse envy and that in homophobic cultures emotionally frank behaviour by men often causes enmity. Altogether, the opportunity to talk about such things in a relaxed manner does seem to reduce the strain on him. Naturally, I remain very circumspect and take great care not to offend him. He makes a fragile impression in the way he comes across, and his depressive symptoms take a long time to improve even with the medication I prescribed for him. His condition worries me, and although he insists that he would never go so far, I am not sure whether he might not attempt to take his own life.

These fears are gradually allayed by the way things develop therapeutically. Johann displays greater security and optimism. He has become more active and at the same time much calmer. He starts to apply for suitable jobs. It looks as if our sessions have given him greater self-confidence and initiative. After fifteen sessions, he tells me he has been through a crisis like this before, after completing his school-leaving exams. At the time, he was treated with similar medication and therapeutic interviews by a psychotherapist, but he feels better looked-after with me: "You have a reputation as a specialist for young academics," he says. At first, I feel flattered, but then hit on the idea that Johann may be creating a narcissistic mirror-world for himself.

I am struck by the intense irritation he displays if I am of a different opinion or do not confirm what he says outright. When I stop functioning as a perfect mirror, I turn into a malevolent persecutor. That puts me on a par with all the teachers, trainers, and professors who have failed to recognise his unusual talents and sought to bring about his downfall. Although he protests that he is grateful for my decision to accept him for therapy, he says it makes him "very sceptical" that we have not solved all his problems although we have been meeting for three months now. For him, his crisis is a "black hole" in his career that he will never be able to make up for.

He speculates whether I might have been subtly urging him to send off job applications as a kind of occupational therapy. He tells me that he does not want to drown in work like "all the others" because he "was born for other things". I become aware that my patient's arrogance is gradually getting to me and making me feel devalued. My reaction is correspondingly irritable, and I tell him pretty bluntly that I can see no reason why he should be spared the strain and stress of everyday life that everyone else has to go through. His gifts may well have made life easier for him up to now, but he might quite simply have to learn to deal with imperfections and to grow as a result. While I feel that in the spirit of cognitive therapy I have a right to correct the unrealistic convictions he entertains ("success without working for it"), my irritation gives me pause. What we have here is an aspect of the therapeutic relationship that is generally called transference and countertransference. The term refers to a process in which, in therapy, the patient unconsciously enacts conflicts from his life-world and "transfers" them to the therapist. In countertransference, the therapist reacts—again unconsciously—to the patient's conflicts.

In this phase of treatment, Johann has much to say about his dreams of a career in music. He watches videos of great musicians and waxes lyrical about a life in the service of music. Although he only practises twice a week for half an hour, he believes that one day he will be able to play like Pablo Casals. In some ill-defined way, I still feel annoyed, then I realise that this is a case of narcissistic transference–countertransference. Behind a façade of mutual confirmation, I now sense more clearly how intensive and influential Johann's fantasies of his own grandeur actually are and how they tie in with his contempt for others. They go hand in hand with a lack of empathy and an extreme sensitivity to criticism. Initially, I had focused exclusively on the patient's fragile sense of self-esteem and, accordingly, had given him the confirmation and protection needed to bolster his feelings of personal value.

From the outset, the therapeutic relationship had revolved around an accept–confirm–support constellation. Given Johann's narcissistic vulnerability, this might have given him greater trust and security.

However, alongside the unspecific interview-therapeutic, resource-orientated, and cognitive–behavioural strategies, it could well be that a species of narcissistic alliance also played a role in improving the situation for him. After twenty-five sessions, the depressive symptoms are significantly assuaged but, at the same time, the range of conflicts with his own personality stand out more starkly. My attunement to the patient's ideas of grandeur has brought about an improvement, but now that same attunement represents the biggest obstacle to further therapy.

Psychoanalytic aspects assert themselves. Johann passes on to me feelings and thoughts that I have to work on in order to understand them. I realise, for example, that his narcissistic self-stylisation is designed to protect him from an insufficiency of recognition. But this gets him trapped in a vicious circle because his self-idealisation is so closely bound up with his devaluation of everyone else. Naturally, these others respond with rejection, which, in its turn, exacerbates his suspicion and isolation. I ask him whether his subtle arrogance is a compensation for the lack of recognition. This intervention gives him pause and he remembers his father. He had achieved much and enjoyed a high reputation as a physicist. "Maybe my contempt is only superficial and I envy him," says Johann. "But if envy makes you look down on others, they will withdraw. Loneliness is the result." It is understandable that one should develop fantasies about one's own significance in order to protect oneself, I add. But the price for this self-protection is high. It leads to ever greater suspicion and loneliness.

The time has come to take a closer look at Johannes' fantasies about the nature of our relationship. At the same time, I attempt to understand my own reactions to the way he is trying to shape that relationship. Initially, I unconsciously took up his narcissistic idealisation. I identified with him; I could empathise and provide him with positive mirroring. Then I became aware that working on his narcissistic conflicts necessarily involved perception of, and reflection on, the feelings of significant others. This made my annoyance understandable, an annoyance that frequently took hold of me without warning. It required an analysis of my own feelings to show me how withering and contemptuous my patient's attitude was to the people he met. This enabled me to better understand the negative responses of, say, his fellow students. Yet, at the same time, I was still able to see the fragile, attachment-seeking side of his character, and I was better able to control my irritable responses, which had been masquerading as confrontational therapeutic technique and might well have ended up jeopardising the therapeutic relationship itself.

The psychodynamic stage of treatment brings an appreciable change in the therapeutic relationship. Interventions of a structural nature modifying behaviour and taking place on the cognitive plane fade into the background. My actively supportive, confirming, and problem-solving attitude changes to concentration on the patient's internal psychic conflicts. Encouraged by this openly creative approach and the acceptance of unconscious conflicts implicit in it, Johann starts exploring his feelings and fantasies *vis-à-vis* his mother. So far, she had appeared solely as an active, regulating, omnipresent, infinitely available figure. But now the patient engages with his inner psychic image of his mother. My impression is that he has been so bound up with her that he can hardly take a step back and see her properly.

He tells me he feels very close to his mother and that even today (as in his childhood) the idea uppermost in his mind is that if she should die, he would have to take his own life. "Strictly speaking," he says, "my mother is the only person who really knows and loves me." As my patient tells me all this, a strange shudder descends on me in countertransference. The therapeutic relationship has become empathic in a profounder sense. I experience feelings similar to the patient's but also feelings that (significant) others experience in his company, feelings that he might experience himself if he did not have to suppress them.

In the following sessions, we work on his relationship with his mother. On the one hand, he is fascinated by the perfection and the glamour of the relationship, on the other, he can readily imagine how his father must have felt excluded and devalued, and why he took refuge in work, television, and alcohol. I also receive a very graphic impression of the envy and ill-humour felt by his school comrades when they clapped eyes on their gifted fellow-student in the company of his mother. Gradually, Johann begins to see the destructive aspects of this glorious symbiosis. He experiences how such close contact weakens him and restricts his potential relations with others. He recalls his first girlfriend and her inability to get through to him. She broke off with him because he permanently made her feel she was beneath him. His mother was greatly relieved when they split up, saying that she was sure he could find "something better". It is probably true that his mother is still "the only woman in his life".

Johann develops the fantasy of a mother–child relationship full of lightness and grace that is as heart-warming as a Renaissance painting. With disarming frankness, he confesses that for many years his favourite occupations had been contemplating photos from his childhood and looking at himself in the mirror. At the same time, he recalls the impulse he felt to simply jump out of the window when someone or something offended him. At first, it does not occur to him that for his mother—and, of course, for his father—this would have been a dreadful tragedy. Only after we have spent quite some time working on his biography and important events in his life does he begin to perceive his mother as an individual in her own right. He starts doubting whether it was a good thing that he should have outshone all the others as mother's "one and all". It scares him that he should have been able to so completely phase out the negative sides of this idealisation.

Johann begins to understand why he and his mother were such an "ideal couple". Her family circumstances had been extremely precarious. The fact that her father had spent some time in prison was never talked about. At home, poverty ruled, which was both bitter in itself and also humiliating. There was hardly ever enough to eat, the children's clothes were shabby, and at school she was victimised and shunned by the other children for that reason. Her marriage was an escape from misery. However, she felt permanently tainted and initially sought to offset that by bringing up her daughter to be a perfect little woman. She, however, soon turned out to be headstrong and recalcitrant, so that Johann advanced to the status of "star" of the family. Everything had to be perfect, clothing, music, schoolwork, behaviour. He was proud when his mother was proud of him, and she was proud when he shone. Contacts with people outside the family were regarded suspiciously, friends were immediately assumed to be a bad influence. Even today, every new acquaintance is a potential enemy to be regarded with profound distrust.

At this stage of the proceedings, in which Johann is recalling biographical experiences and the feelings that go with them, the therapeutic relationship is highly complex. Patient and therapist take turns to play very different roles: child, mother, father, girlfriend and friend, rival and enemy. In this theatre of the psyche, they are both improvising agents and critical observers, sometimes trying, like authors and directors, to give the game a new twist.

In the concluding stages, Johann starts thinking about his professional prospects. Another central topic is his desire for a relationship and what it should look like. Although he is outwardly quite stable and optimistic, there is much that I feel has not been sorted out. We cannot continue with therapy because his job takes him too far away. I remain in telephone contact with him for a while, until his fears in connection with starting a new job have subsided. He quickly finds new, superficial friends (as he calls them). "But it's better that way," he says, "clearly defined, no strings attached." I was rather worried about my patient and feared that he might decompensate when the next setback struck. Accordingly, I advised him to seek further treatment at his new location, not least because short-term therapy can resolve an immediate crisis but cannot get to the root of personality problems.

At the follow-up three years after conclusion of therapy, Johann is more reserved than most of my other patients. Although he would prefer not to be reminded of the crisis he had been through, he is still grateful for the help he received. Asked what he thought it was that helped him, he summarises as follows: the regular appointments that he initially rejected and my own "laid-back" attitude gave him security. He had been in despair and our encounters and exchanges gave him hope. He gives the significance of the therapeutic relationship (A) a score of six. Probably my advice in connection with his behaviour (B) also had a stabilising effect, and he was able to see many things from a different perspective (C). These two dimensions are given five points each. Initially, he found engaging with his own past "pretty weird", but, in retrospect, he sees its importance and now pays greater heed to his feelings, "odd fantasies", and dreams. This now helps him to understand himself and others. Accordingly, he gives the psychodynamic dimension (D) seven points. Through concern for his emotional conflicts, he is now in a better position to express annoying feelings more appropriately, especially when he feels slighted and offended. Perhaps this is why he now finds it easier to tolerate his partner's moods: "Now I know that I'm not always easy to stomach either." His crisis and the treatment for it opened his eyes to the fact that things cannot always run "super-smoothly". It also helps him be more tolerant of crises and imperfections encountered in his job. "And another thing," he says. "Who knows if without therapy I'd even still be alive?" In his own words he describes the existential dimension (E) of psychotherapy as follows: "An opportunity to face up to oneself and one's relationships unmasked. Without resonance it can't be done." He gives this dimension ten points.

Histrionic personality traits: a student in search of constant thrills

"There has to be glitz and glamour"

Christian comes to see me because of an ill-defined feeling of vacuity and despair. Although as a student he is quite successful, he feels that his life is pointless. Sometimes, he thinks it would be "chic" to take his own life: "I am completely alone." He has no difficulty making contact with others, but after a while everything turns stale and tedious. "When I see a fantastic-looking woman, it bowls me over completely," he says. But after the first few exchanges, the glamour disappears: "I hear myself talking and it sounds vapid." He often has the impression of acting on a stage and not really being there. He does not know whether he is exaggerating his feelings and making a drama out of everything or whether he really has a problem. Even his thoughts of suicide do not feel authentic: "I don't know how close I am to doing it."

At the first few sessions, Christian describes his life in glowing colours. It is easy to establish a trustful relationship and he appears to find the interviews beneficial. He also feels accepted and acknowledged: "My self-esteem is coming back ..." In the third session, he recounts the following dream:

I'm lying in a meadow, everything around me has a bluish tinge. The sky is purple, vampire-like female creatures with very erotic bodies come close, everything is fine. I have a feeling of weightlessness.

After this account, he tells me of a girlfriend who is not really his girlfriend. Although they have sex, neither of them wants a steady relationship. His girlfriend, especially, wants to be free more than anything else; he admires her self-reliance. She has frequent affairs and tells him about them in detail. Although he finds this arousing, at the same time he feels uncomfortable, sometimes vaguely disgusted: "She's a book written by lots of others, I can only add some notes."

When I ask him whether it is a coincidence that he should have chosen a sex partner who is not interested in an attachment, the following image suggests itself to him: "I'm like a small plant that can't grow because of all the big tree trunks with their big crowns." I suggest that he might be frightened by his own vitality and power if he presented himself as a big tree with a splendid crown.

This reminds Christian of his father, whom he frequently feared for his aggression and impulsiveness. His mother also suffered from his father's outbursts of anger; on occasion he even struck her. Yet, after such altercations, she would go to bed with him: "Disgusting, I often asked her why she didn't divorce him." Later, she disclosed to him that his father was sexually passive and liked to be overwhelmed. Christian, too, seeks the darker side of sexuality. He has long been intrigued by pornographic films. While he is seriously afraid of being "somehow perverted" by pornography, the genitals of copulating couples fascinate him. Paradoxically, he finds something pure and clear in these couplings. Because in the porn films he identifies with women who "get taken", he sometimes thinks he might be gay.

One session is particularly worthy of note. At the beginning, Christian tells me about exclusive bars where the patrons orbit around each other in a hall of mirrors. He has met a young woman he might fall in love with, but feels a "strange fear". When he thinks of her, a pornographic scene occurs to him: two men having an orgasm at the same time while indulging in oral and vaginal sex with a woman. Christian sees another scene in his mind's eye, a woman who grows old while she has sex with him: "She withers away and has to die, like a rose eaten out from the inside by a worm." As he speaks, I have the opposite image: "A woman made to blossom like a rose by her lover."

I tell Christian about this: he says he can imagine it, but his feeling is different.

He recalls the following dream:

> My grandmother has died, I'm sitting at her bedside. I feel sad, but her death is not as chilling as I always thought it would be.

Christian finds this dream very odd because his grandmother is still hale and hearty. She has, however, told him that she greatly misses her own mother and for that reason has no objection to dying soon. Christian changes the subject and tells me that his parents always quarrel at Christmas-time. Father has his knife into Mother's family because they are so "dreadfully" untidy. Her sister, he says, is a "slut". In my mind's eye, I see Christian and his father simultaneously attracted and intimidated by loose women. I ask him whether he has similar feelings to his father and prefers to keep women at arm's length for aesthetic reasons. He thinks it over and then says, "Maybe that's why I'm so lonely."

After the session, Christian has a dream:

> I've gone home after a dispute at work and sit on my mother's lap for protection.

He cannot stand any kind of conflict and calls himself incredibly sensitive. On the other hand, there have been times when he would gladly have "hit someone in the face if they looked at him sideways". I suggest that the reason he might find it so difficult to approach women and get on with his colleagues at work is that he reacts to minor slurs with extreme anger. He tells me that in puberty he was a real tearaway. The motto he and a friend thought up was "Skate and Destroy", and he dreamt of skateboarding right into the middle of a crowd with no thought for casualties: "And what do I end up doing? Joining the civil service!"

He asks himself how his father came to terms with anger and resentment. It occurs to him that his father's constant "hectic activity" in the garden at every opportunity might have been his way of controlling his impulses. Communing with nature was all very well, but it also stopped him from making contacts. Then Christian gives me a florid account of how, after Sunday breakfast, he and his mother would linger at table talking animatedly about art and literature:

"Outside, Father scurries past the window, sweating, with grimy hands. I give him a lordly wave." In this scene I sense something provocative that is angled at me as well. At the same time, I think of Christian's worries about growing up, committing himself to a job, and asserting himself in the outside world. So I tell him that perhaps he is afraid to go his own way and step out of his father's negative shadow in which he finds a mirror of himself. He says, "One minute I'm reading *The Magic Mountain*, and the next I go out on the street looking for someone I can bash in the face!"

Suddenly, I recall the "cool" relationship between Christian and his girlfriend. Does it perhaps also fill him with rage, annoyance, and disappointment, which he does his best to conceal behind a façade of cosmopolitan tolerance? While I dwell on these thoughts, he tells me the following story. "When I was a boy, I had a cloth June bug to play with, and one day, I don't know why, I threw it down the lavatory and pulled the chain. After that I was very sad. The June bug was no longer there. My aunt bought me the same June bug; for a while I believed she had found it somewhere a long way away." Lavatories, he said, had always fascinated him. He had not wanted to get rid of the June bug. Perhaps, even as a small child, he had started experimenting with separation and death.

Christian tells me he has been familiar with "this strange sadness of saying goodbye" for as long as he can remember. His grandfather died when he was four, around the time of the June bug episode. He withdrew into a world of his own. Only when he was thirteen or fourteen and his maternal grandmother died did he become fully aware of how terrible death really is. I say that perhaps the June bug game was a way of deluding himself into believing that he could make things disappear and then bring them back again. This worked when he was four, but no longer when he was thirteen or fourteen. "Yes," he replies, "when my grandmother died, it brought home to me how powerless we are in the face of death. Perhaps that's why I take such an interest in death, to create an aesthetic distance that makes my feelings less intensive and painful. When you talk or philosophise about death, it recedes into the distance. But when the light starts failing, I feel the organic side of me, this uncanny awareness that we all have to die."

On his way to my practice, he passes an old, wrought iron gate overgrown with ivy. It gives him the feeling that certain things last, that there is something "beyond time". It makes his pain "easier to bear". He tells me of the following dream:

> I was invited to a girlfriend's birthday party. It was a very large house; I arrived late. The party was in full swing, all over the house. I go up and down endless staircases. Then I suddenly find myself in a sauna where the others are having a great time. I see a girlfriend giving someone head. I feel out of place, as if I don't belong. Then I encounter thousands of yogis, and I go off in search of the birth-day girl. We kiss and her lipstick peels off. Suddenly, I know that this is not real love. After that I fall down the stairs backwards. I don't want the others to see me like that and don't want them to be there. I wake up feeling disorientated. What am I doing here? I ask myself.

The rich imagery of the dream confuses me somewhat, but, as I listen, the subject of birth starts occupying the foreground. Christian associates very little with these events; I have the feeling that he is expecting some kind of reward for having had such a "brilliant dream". So I tell him about my birth scenario. Surprised, he answers that only the day before he had been imagining what his birth might have been like. His mother says she was greatly looking forward to it, but Christian has his doubts. It occurs to him that perhaps his corus-cating erotic enactments were a way of reviving his early relationship with a mother he experienced as distractingly beautiful. She has all kinds of treasures that she shares only with him. He frequently longs for a powerful woman who "would free me from all hurts and inad-equacies". But he finds it harder to imagine touching the hand of a woman he is attracted to than to think of himself taking part in a violent sex orgy. He recalls his own vulnerability. He thinks about how precious his boy's room in his parents' house is to him, where all the details must never be changed. "You have to preserve some of that security for yourself," he says.

During this period, Christian concludes his medical studies with very good grades and finds it increasingly easy to imagine what made his father become a specialist in internal medicine. The scorn for his father's manic gardening activity appears to be on the wane. He has another dream:

> I enter a medieval tower, the stairs are made of old wood, it's nice and welcom-ing, but it all smells of decay. There is someone there with a drug wrapped in parchment. I know that if I take this drug it will kill me, but it still exerts an irre-sistible attraction on me. High up on the stairs is a woman, and I'm sure she'll

be mine if I take the drug. On the ground floor of the tower I see a half-putre-fied figure. It's just lying there, green and rotting. Then I go up the stairs to the young naked woman and I kiss her between the legs; it tastes very good, but, at the same time, she is cold as a fish. Her flesh is not warm but it is exciting. Then I wait for the drug to work because I know it will kill me. I see time slipping by like sand in an hourglass.

With reference to the dream, Christian tells me he sometimes fears waking up in case he has turned into an old man while he was asleep. Perhaps sexual adventures can help us to ignore the reality of death, he says.

In this phase of therapy, Christian meets a young woman who has fallen in love with him and would not hesitate to embark on a serious relationship. Christian, however, holds back, telling me that his "aesthetics of pornography" prevents him from wholeheartedly responding to his new girlfriend's overtures. After we have spent some time reflecting on why he finds his girlfriend wanting and is more attracted by women who already have a steady relationship, I say, "You seem to find it hard to stomach the fact that there are attractive women who are not available; for example, because they have someone else." Yes, he says, he does tend to feel that every alluring woman has some kind of treasure within her, something new and enticing "that I want to get hold of, perhaps even destroy, so that no one else can have it." I tell him that his envy is preventing him from embarking on a uniquely loving relationship. It would, of course, mean forgoing his "unlimited" possibilities. He would also have to acknowledge that his youth is not eternal. After this intervention, Christian has the idea that he can only remain an "eternal talent" as long as he has not achieved anything: "That way, I evade the effects of time, but it also arrests me in my development."

Christian's therapy is coming to a close (after eighty sessions), and the topics we have been addressing reflect that fact. We, too, have no choice but to go our different ways. Christian appears to be caught up in an internal tussle between progress and retreat. On the one hand, he displays greater commitment to his relationship with his girlfriend; on the other, he still likes to withdraw into confidential *tête-à-têtes* with his mother in which he tells her about his sexual affairs and she listens with a knowing smile on her face. He also feels more comfortable with me than with his girlfriend, though he tells me that their relationship is deepening in "really quite a gratifying way". His visits to her parents are, however, unpalatable, because they are so "dreadfully middle-class". It is the same old story all over again: "mummy, daddy, kids". He escapes to his former girlfriend, who gives him a "sexual kick" without any talk of love and commitment. It makes him feel great when his girlfriend calls him in the morning and he's still in bed with his ex with condoms lying around everywhere. I suggest that he may be carrying on with his ex-girlfriend because he is afraid of being hurt and disappointed. He says: "I know it's an awful breach of trust, but there's nothing I can do about it."

Towards the end of therapy, Christian engages with separation at various different levels: infant longings, delusions of erotic grandeur, distressing fantasies. One of Goethe's famous sayings has stuck in his head: "You can't bring them up without making anyone suffer." Adulthood is painful and risky, but freedom makes it all worth it. I notice that Christian has become altogether more active, displaying astonishing commitment to a social institution he supports. He begins to enjoy the steady relationship with his girlfriend, rather than seeing it as a "fun-killer". He is able to concentrate on his work, and his dissertation is almost finished. Summing up, he says that the feeling of "living behind a sheet of Perspex or on a stage" has gone away.

In our last session, we come back to his first dream, in which he was lying in a field feeling sexually desired by fascinating extra-terrestrial females. At the time, he had felt that the world was going past him like a film: "a world without me". Now he feels bound up in the progress of time. Looking at an old Dutch still-life shortly before, he no longer found the subject of transience frightening, as he had previously. "It's the way things are," he says, "first the blossom, then the fresh green fruit, and finally ripeness and decay." Like the ivy on the old gates that he sees on his way to our sessions. "You don't have to see death as an inferno, you can see it as a womb to return to." My feeling is that with this patient my work has been interesting and important. Much has remained unaddressed, but I feel hopeful that the patient can turn the impulses he has received to account and develop further. In retrospect, he says our exchanges have helped him find his way to his own self. In what way? I ask. His answer: "Trust, talking, being understood, dreaming, recognising covert feelings and no longer being afraid of love."

From my point of view, the central elements in this case were the existential aspects (E). Acceptance of the restrictions placed on all human agency and ambition was an existential constant. Insight into relational conflicts and understanding of the attendant emotions also played a crucial role (D), the ambivalence of proximity and distance, attachment and passion, envy and gratitude. Ultimately, Christian was able to understand these conflicts in terms of both his present situation and his biography. He achieved a mentalization of what had formerly been diffuse emotions and experiences. This new awareness can be regarded both as a depth-psychological and as a cognitive aspect of treatment (C). The role played by behaviourally orientated advice (B) and supportive dimensions of the helpful alliance (A) was subordinate. However, it took the therapeutic encounter as a resonant space to open the door to existential understanding in the first place (A, E, A). Here, things come full circle in our ABCDE model.

Fifteen years after concluding psychotherapy, I call Christian and ask him for a retrospective assessment of his treatment. His spontaneous response is that he has good memories of it and is still grateful that he "could sort out the things that were getting to me". Initially, his reluctance to embark on psychotherapy had been considerable, but soon the whole thing had been a liberating experience. "I'm more alive now than I was," he says. "I still have to find out who I am, but now I'm much calmer about it all." Professionally, he also enjoys discovering new things; self-realisation is no problem in the big specialist practice. His loving partner is also a source of stimulus and joy. "The therapy still helps me to live my life more consciously," he says.

At the end of our follow-up, I ask Christian to assess the various categories in the ABCDE model. The general feeling of being accepted and supported (A) receives a score of eight on the scale from zero (not important) to ten (supremely important). Behavioural aspects (B) played a minor role, he awards six points for that. Christian gives C (intellectual engagement with views, attitudes, and values) eight points. Awareness of conflicts and biographical entanglements (D) was also an important feature and is given nine points. Especially important for Christian was the general feeling of being understood and responded to (E). Accordingly, he gives this dimension a "straight ten". The trusting atmosphere in particular had helped him to accept his contradictory inclinations with respect to freedom, sexuality, and creativity.

Impulse control disorder with Don Juan syndrome: an architect intends to shoot himself

"Only when I feel the radiance of pleasure do I exist"

R ichard, a fifty-year-old architect, approaches me for help because his wife has "inexplicably" left him after years of marriage. The marriage was largely loveless and he has always had affairs, but this new development has knocked him sideways. His feelings veer between consuming rage and debilitating sorrow. Following an inner compulsion, he takes his hunting gun out of its cabinet every night and sticks the barrel in his mouth "to make an end of things". Then he thinks of his children and puts the gun away again: "A drink or two always bring me to my senses, it's a help."

At the first interview, the contrast with this desperate account of his situation on the phone could hardly be starker. Richard is suave and self-possessed. He talks of his success as an architect, his energy, his capacity for hard work. "The only problem," he says, "is that I always try to please everyone." He is genuinely committed and helpful, selflessly supporting various social institutions. In my presence, he takes immense care to capture and hold my attention and has little difficulty in doing so. His stories about himself are colourful, original, and immaculately tasteful. However, soon I have the impression that his fascinating account of himself is an attempt to engage my sympathy. As he chats on entertainingly, I begin to sense the helplessness and despair beneath the surface. I feel an urge to put my arms round him and assure him of my solidarity. As the interview wears on, the pressure on him increases; he becomes extremely fidgety, twists his hands, and stares at me with wide-open eyes. He asks me whether sedatives might not be a good idea.

Richard tells me that in the past he has benefited from autogenic training, so I show him some tension and relaxation exercises. Mindful of the "mood swings" he is subject to, we work out a carefully conceived plan for his everyday routines and discuss behaviours that can help prevent his impulses from running away with him. Especially in the evenings, when he often feels as if he has "fallen into a hole and can't get back out", it is important for him to have reassuring rituals to fall back on that are designed to help him "find his way back to himself". We discuss the books and the music that might help him think about his relational conflicts with greater equanimity. My impression is that, deep down, my patient knows all this but is unable to use this knowledge in coming to terms with the present crisis. He is grateful for my suggestions and acts upon them, but the main thing is "to have someone to talk to". He accepts my advice to keep his children in mind and not do anything irreversible. We plan joint activities for him with the children; ultimately, it is his responsibility for them that holds him back from committing suicide. In thinking more about his children's needs, he also becomes more mindful of his own feelings.

After these initial crisis meetings, we agree on a brief course of psychotherapy. Alongside the advice on regulating his behaviour, discussion of his "strange attitudes" plays a central role. "I always do everything," he says, "but I never suffice." Criticism, however piffling, immediately throws him off balance. If something does not function from the outset, everything is worthless. He intensifies his unhappiness with dark fantasies and cogitations: "If I'm heading for disaster anyway, I might as well do it properly." He is often so angry that it "takes his breath away". I have the feeling that Richard is alone with his anger and that he is losing contact with me. We find out that it gives him a feeling of great intensity when he gives his anger its head and really lets go. At the same time, it also propels him into a state of self-destructive isolation. After a while, he refers to this as a "strange substitute for passion". Discussing topics like these has a calming influence on him. He says he feels "somehow sustained" by our exchanges.

After about ten sessions, another topic comes to the fore. He deceived his wife right at the beginning of their marriage. He says he finds women "just tremendous" and is proud of his sexual prowess. "I make them all happy," he claims. He stresses that he never plays rough but is always at pains to give women profound pleasure with his amorous skills. Among his girlfriends is a woman who has a steady relationship. She meets Richard because with him she can experience things that her partner cannot give her. Richard is glad to be of service. Oddly enough, the image that presents itself to me is that of an abandoned child feeling all alone in a strange world. Richard tells me more about his exploits. "When I see their eyes shining," he says, "I feel that I exist." Despite the self-possessed tone with which he tells me this, he makes an oddly timid, vulnerable impression on me. He says of himself that he only feels relaxed when he has made a woman happy. Then he feels he has a right to be alive. "It's all about love, appreciation, and power," he says. After a while, it occurs to him that perhaps it is also about taming "the female animal". At bottom, women are dangerous: "The best way of keeping them at bay is sex." In this stage of therapy, we begin to identify the biographical roots his destructive anxieties and constructive coping strategies stem from.

Richard tells me that he always found his mother very unapproachable. He cannot remember her ever having smiled at him. One brother, who was twelve months old at the time, died a year before he was born. Since that time his mother had probably suffered from severe depression. His father was inwardly crippled by the war and a long period of captivity. "There was never an emotional relationship between us," Richard tells me. At the age of two and a half, Richard became severely ill and believes he can remember how he opened the flap of a kind of incubator to touch the little girl lying next to him. After the birth of another brother, who was four years younger, he was put into a children's home because his mother had had a stroke during childbirth. That was the time when, on an outing, he fell into a pond and almost drowned. He can still remember his mortal fear and the resuscitation process. Then he caught a dangerous infection and would have died if, at the very last moment, his father had not collected him from the children's home and taken him to a hospital.

At school, he realised that being an achiever earned him respect from the others, yet he still felt somehow alien. It took masturbation for him to achieve "a feeling for myself". He was never able to "work up any real affection" for his friends, male or female. As an architecture student at university, he dreamt of achieving something "really important". Ultimately, he did indeed succeed in acquiring a good professional reputation but he also developed inhibitions about being as aggressive as the situation demanded. In professional disputes, he would "back down" and suppress his anger. Martial sports were helpful in this respect but on the career ladder he let himself be overtaken by colleagues who had a great deal less to offer than he did. He became something of a loner, a development that he is not unhappy about because he has come far without "sucking up to others". And he can still "drive a woman out of her mind". In the past few years, his work has taken up most of his life. Apart from his "little lovey-doveys", all his friends and acquaintances come from his own professional circle. At home he was more like a guest. He had "no really close relationship" with his children. They were looked after by his wife; he was the breadwinner.

We elaborate the following explanations for his conflicts: due to depression and the consequences of a stroke, his mother was unable to lavish much affection on him. This defect is like a wound that he used his talents to compensate for. His absentee father was also unable to give him anything much in the way of secure bonding and recognition. As a boy, the primal trust he was able to develop was rudimentary. Soon he learnt to employ his creative abilities to "fake his way around" loneliness and despair. Traumatic experiences aroused mortal fears in him and exacerbated his vulnerability. In puberty, sexuality gave him access to his own feelings. Yet, in view of his infant attachment disorder and the difficulty he had in stomaching disappointment, he found it difficult to enter into emotionally sustaining relationships. He let down important friends, both male and female, and, in turn, was let down by them. In his marriage with a self-reliant, possibly rather unemotional woman, he re-enacted the "loveless attachment" scenario in a relationship increasingly marred by mutual devaluation, letting himself be degraded to the status of an unloved and frequently scorned provider. He compensated for this with the titillation supplied by his numerous love affairs. His unenthusiastic acquittal of his duties as husband and father ultimately turned his wife and his children against him. He was long unaware of the fact that he had played an active part in these developments. We discovered that the facts listed here were the reasons why he was unable to react to situational conflicts with the degree of aggression that they merited. On the one hand, sexual skill and prowess in extramarital relationships were a compensation for the lack of emotional depth experienced at home. But when his girlfriends wanted more from him than mere sex, he was assailed by violent fears of lapsing into a bout of depression. There is no alternative for him but to make good his escape, but this, in turn, exacerbates the torments of loneliness and despair.

In one session, Richard tells me about a new conquest. They have met a number of times and had "good sex". The woman has admitted her affection for him, even going so far as to talk of love. "That's something I can't stand at any price," he says. "I've told her never to say 'I love you' ever again!" He lapses into a kind of trance. "I feel trapped in the spider's web of love, it's like being eaten alive," he says. "It's like it was with my mother, she drags me down into the depths like a millstone. It's like quicksand, a bog that won't let go of me . . . drowning in amniotic fluid or mother's milk." Emerging from his trance, he says, rather more calmly, that love is a weapon that stops people from dealing sensibly with one another. Perhaps that is why he cannot get away from his wife: "There was no love there."

As I listen to Richard, my feelings are mixed. I sense how our exchanges give him greater stability, and the more dramatic his narratives become during the session, the more circumspectly he can go about putting his life in order. After such emotional culminations, our exchanges also regain their composure, and Richard uses them to engage with existential topics like the rival claims of attachment and passion. He has started painting again in the evenings instead of slumping into a chair with a bottle of wine to watch television all night. At his fitness studio, he has found—"if you'll excuse the expression"—a "new fuck". He has started going out "openly" with Susanne. Who knows, "maybe something will come of it".

After twenty-five sessions, the acute crisis is over. Thoughts of suicide have faded away. Richard decides to continue with the therapy in the form of psychoanalytic treatment. He wants to understand his emotions and, thus, protect himself from uncontrolled impulses. And he wants to respond to the feelings of others with less anxiety: "Regular appointments, a reliable setting, human understanding, that all helps."

Further treatment takes place in two sessions a week with the patient on the couch. Richard uses the couch setting to devote himself unrestrictedly to his experiences, thoughts and feelings. He is still very imaginative and witty, so that I am sometimes in danger of over-looking the extent of his distress. His intelligent humour is a special gift that helps him in coping with difficult experiences. On the other hand, his desire to be entertaining and never to get on anyone's nerves makes him neglect his own needs. Those needs are pent up and vent themselves in outbreaks of anger that he himself is at a loss to under-stand. This is characteristic both of his personal and professional rela-tions. Accordingly, therapy focuses on his ambivalence about entering into genuine involvements. His relationship with Susanna is steady and he enjoys having an affectionate, albeit demanding, woman at his side. Sex is passionate and they both get on well in the practical sides of life. Yet, Richard feels a strange urge to put an end to his relation-ship with her. His ambivalent desires for closeness and snugness make themselves felt in therapy. As soon as the therapeutic process gets down to the meat of things, Richard responds by cancelling appointments or arriving late.

His professional relations are equally ambivalent. He reacts to conflicts by withdrawing in a huff, which does him more harm than good. We understand these responses as a desperate fight for inde-pendence with which he hopes to cope with the fears of abandonment that have assailed him since childhood. Alongside these psycho-analytic interpretations, cognitive interventions continue to play a role. In the face of difficult disputes with his business partner, we dis-cuss elementary rules of successful negotiation: distinguishing emo-tional and factual aspects, asserting interests not ideologies, thinking up options for all involved. These discussions are by no means detri-mental for our conflict-centred therapeutic efforts. On the contrary, Richard feels accepted and supported as a result of the attention we give to his immediate problems. It reinforces his willingness to engage with his unconscious conflicts.

This also becomes apparent in his separation from his wife. She has filed for divorce, which initially knocks Richard sideways. In his emotional confusion, he veers between despondency and impotent rage: "I could smash everything to bits." In our exchanges, Richard regains stability. On the one hand, he finds it helpful to understand the biographical and unconscious background for his disappointment and anger. On the other, he also benefits from our concrete considerations about how he can manage the separation with minimal distress for all concerned.

Neither is psychoanalysis in any way impaired by behavioural interventions. Richard is still inclined to drown his sorrows in alcohol. I remind him of the strategies we devised at the beginning of his therapy, strategies he has since found helpful. He remembers how important it is in such situations to gain time and pit positive impulses against the temptation. One highly effective ploy is very simple: first drink a glass of water and talk things over with someone. Tatyana supports him in this, and even when the mood takes him, he succeeds in restricting himself to two glasses of wine. On many days, he drinks no alcohol at all. He finds this important, as he has noticed that he can no longer take as much alcohol as he could before. On evenings when he is alone, detailed planning helps him desist from "indulging": sport, reading, listening to music. He has also taken out his easel again and started painting so as to "have something I can hold on to".

As things stand, Richard has his destructive impulses under control. In an interim summing-up, he says he feels he has started getting back on top of his life. Although still distressed, he feels encouraged and optimistic thanks to therapy. He imagines that working on his psychic problems could lead to a "diversity of experience" that will enrich his life and make things "turn out well". I, too, hope that his new creativity in organising his life will make it easier for him to be mindful of himself and others. He finds the integrative model interesting and evaluates the significance of the individual dimensions as follows: A 10, B 7, C 8, D 8, E 7.

After reading my report on his treatment, Richard sends me an email: "Pretty accurate, almost frighteningly on target. But I can't quite suppress a grin: the entanglements, the compulsions, the confusions, the theatre of the soul, the compensation mechanisms . . . In the last resort it's encouraging that despite, or because of, all the soul-searching, life ends up all the richer for it."

Severe depression plus burnout: a company employee is completely burnt out and sees no hope for himself

"They took the ground away from under my feet"

Wolfgang is a fifty-five-year-old company employee who likes to be called "Wolf". Reorganisation by his firm has reduced his status to that of a marginal figure. He feels offended, hurt, and humiliated. A feeling of helplessness has taken hold of him: "They've taken the ground away from under my feet." Within a few weeks, he experiences a serious bout of depression and lapses into increasing despair: "I feel completely changed." He is cut off from his own feelings: "I'm no longer myself." He sees no prospects for the future and tosses and turns all night, unable to sleep: "In the morning I'm absolutely worn out." Since the onset of his depression he has been drinking too much, one large bottle of wine a day, sometimes more. This is something he has never experienced before. He prefers "not to face up to" the question of how serious his thoughts of suicide are. He sought the advice of a psychiatrist. The supportive exchanges with his doctor and treatment with antidepressive drugs and sleeping pills were helpful to a certain extent, but after months of treatment he still "sees no light at the end of the tunnel".

His psychiatrist was committed to his cause, even writing a letter to the company management complaining about the way his patient had been treated. After almost nine months off sick, the company offers to pension him off ahead of time. He is uncertain whether this "would do me good and take the pressure off me". On the other hand, the pension he would receive at this stage in his career would be insufficient for him "to make ends meet". He opts in favour of a new course of psychotherapy.

At the first few sessions, Wolf appears very despondent and is unable to "find one spark of value in me". Like my psychiatrist colleague before me, I do my best to be supportive and free him from the pressures of self-accusation. While he readily accepts suggestions on how to give his everyday life a clearer structure, he finds it very hard to put them into practice. In an attempt to find a starting point for a change in behaviour, I enquire into his resources. Wolf tells me that he used to be a keen swimmer. As with all the other activities that might do him good, his depressive withdrawal has caused him to give up swimming completely. Accordingly, I advise him to start going back to the swimming baths at certain predetermined times. This, I feel, might help impose rhythm on the chaos of his daily life. Sceptical at first, he finally agrees to try it out "for your sake". We also discuss mealtime rituals, which he used to find important: "Now I just gulp down junk food."

After three weeks of therapy with two sessions a week, I encourage Wolf to accept his company's offer of light work on an hourly basis, expecting this to impose more order on his daily routines. It takes time for him to re-accustom himself to regular hours, but he manages to spend a few hours in the office rather than staying home and "staring at the ceiling". To his surprise, his colleagues treat him with respect, and there is no cause for him to be "so ashamed that I just want the ground to open up and swallow me". Regular meals are also "quite a good idea". Initially giving up on alcohol "for your sake", he now realises what a good thing this is. In six months he has put on thirty pounds in weight and notices how he has changed when he goes swimming: "I've had enough of life as a fatso."

These changes are, however, only feasible because his appointments are close to one another and he feels "gentle pressure" on my part. Probably he can only relate to my suggestions for altering his behaviour because he feels accepted and understood. The respectful resonance he encounters at our sessions makes it easier for him to comply with my recommendations against his own resistance. Alongside behavioural concerns, we also discuss emotionally significant topics. He feels so degraded by the restructuring scheme that he has not one good word to say about the company and his superiors, though for years he had enjoyed working there: "My work was my home." But now he badmouths everything, the company, the work, his colleagues, and, above all, himself. As a counterpoint, I try to convince him of how much he has achieved. His awareness grows that with his negative thought spirals he has been making himself more and more helpless and "dragging himself down". We set off on a little imaginary journey to sectors where he has achieved much and can be proud of himself. This inspires him to look out old documents at home that were important for his work group. I attempt to sensitise him to the fact that the phone calls and emails he receives from his former colleagues are a reflection of their concern for him and not meant to be in any way objectionable: "They show what a reputation you have."

As I listen to him, I ask myself what has become of the active and rebellious sides of his character. I try to imagine what they might be like. During this inner quest, Wolf surprises me with the news that he has unearthed his old LPs from the late 1960s: *Wind Cries Mary* by Jimi Hendrix, *Blowing in the Wind* by Bob Dylan, *Born to Be Wild* by Steppenwolf. He now no longer drinks in the evenings but dreams himself back to his "wild years". He had long since forgotten them because he was afraid of what might have happened: "How easily I could have slithered down into drink and drugs." During his account, I have the feeling that, inwardly, Wolf has become a little more lively. I myself find that the lethargy that weighed on me in our first few sessions has lightened.

We spend more of our time working with memories and fantasies. Step by step, Wolf manages to extricate himself from his negative self-reinforcement ("if things are bad, they may as well be really and truly bad"). Thoughts of suicide have receded. I have the impression that, in his exchanges with me, he finds a "creative transitional space" in which he can engage with the world and himself.

During the brief course of therapy encompassing twenty-five sessions, the following biographical constellations take centre stage: Wolf is surprised to find that he has no real image of his mother: "I cannot find any inner access to her." Everything is overshadowed by the unpleasant conflicts in puberty. He believes, however, that he was a wanted child. Growing up in Upper Bavaria, he was "of course" given a very Catholic upbringing. His mother was "rather aloof" and regarded everything physical with distaste. Wolf imagines, however, that she could be affectionate and loving. His father was more "casual". At home, he mostly stayed out of things and, as a lawyer, always had a lot of work to do. Their relationship was, however, not bad, and he knows that up to puberty his father was very proud of his "crown prince".

His brother, two years younger than himself, had always been "more unruly". He took a much earlier interest in sex and also felt attracted by criminal circles. On various occasions he came into conflict with the law. Wolf, by contrast, was reasonably well behaved and felt quite happy with his "middle-class childhood". At school, things were more challenging, but he always "scraped through somehow". An initial crisis occurred during puberty. At fourteen, he turned away from the church and the Boy Scouts and started to go his own way. His mother took this amiss and made it very clear that she thought little of the way he was turning out. His father also became increasingly rigid and authoritarian. After leaving school, Wolf broke off all contact with his parents and, out of protest, studied political science. Later, he switched to law. In his time at university, he got involved in a number of very difficult relationships with women. Seen in retrospect, a first marriage that lasted three years and remained childless had never been happy. In his subsequent relationships, he "never struck lucky". Things changed with his second wife. He met her in the USA, they went through some "wild times" together, and, ultimately, she came back to Germany with him. Despite their two daughters, family life soon became unbearable, though Wolf's opinion is that they just "drifted apart". He dropped out of university, and his job became the hub of his life. Today, all his friends and acquaintances still originate from his work environs. This was why he lost all his important contacts when he was pushed out of his job.

After this initial supportive and stabilising phase, complete with behavioural suggestions and the clarification of negative cognitive takes on life, the following conflicts came to the forefront: Wolf becomes aware that he has very ambivalent attitudes to people who represent authority of one kind or another. On the one hand, he longs for recognition; on the other, he flatly rejects anyone who "tries to tell me what to do". He connects these conflicts with his childhood: "I was always trying to earn my mother's affection, but I never had the feeling I was being properly accepted or understood. Perhaps that's why I'm so sensitive to criticism." *Vis-à-vis* his father, he also feels a strange mixture of respect and dislike and cannot find a genuine explanation for this.

At the beginning of therapy, Wolf mentioned the fact that he could never remember his dreams. Acting upon my advice to write them down immediately after waking up, he tells me about the following dream:

> I was caught in the company building at night. I had gone to the toilet although it was 'illegal'. But they were waiting for me and there was no escape. I only had a scruffy pair of underpants on, and my girlfriend was waiting for me outside.

For Wolf, the dream illustrates his feeling of not belonging to the company any more. On the other hand, he feels an urge to uncover the darker sides of the company: "What kind of underhand dealings go on there behind closed doors?" Then he addresses himself: "Where are my dirty and shabby sides, which I conceal although it might be good for me to see them?" The dream triggers a multiplicity of thoughts and feelings. Finally, he enquires into the meaning of his girlfriend waiting outside: "Perhaps I can only really open up to someone when I've done my dirty washing."

This reminds him of his obdurate behaviour in his personal relations. Small differences of opinion are enough to make him withdraw. Another dream is significant in this connection:

> I come home and there's a stranger there who threatens me with a knife. I call for help but don't know if anyone can hear me.

The first thing that occurs to Wolf is his anxieties, but then he recalls his aggressive impulses. His (female) superior, who ousted him out of his position, is a case in point. He feels he could easily kill her. It distresses him to have urges like this. He discovers that he never experiences anger and annoyance directly; they find only suppressed expression, "coming out the back way". He asks himself whether we can afford to engage with such complicated conflicts in the framework of a brief course of therapy. I ask myself the same question.

Towards the end of the brief therapy, we attempt a summing-up. We have succeeded in understanding why he is so ambivalent about authoritative persons. On the one hand, he feels dependent on their appreciation and recognition, which gives him a feeling of security. On the other hand, there is much that makes him angry, but he is incapable of moderating his responses. The only recourse is repression and avoidance. Alongside these psychodynamic aspects, supportive behavioural interventions and the activation of Wolf's creative interests play a significant part. I encourage him to rediscover his rebellious music. I repeatedly suggest that he might take up the guitar again, as playing it had "consoled him in many lonely hours" in puberty. Initially, he found the idea laughable, but soon discovered the extent to which he was more himself when he was playing his instrument. He improvised and lost himself in his memories: "It does you good, like talking to one another here. Just being there, getting a sense of yourself, finding resonance." Sometimes, frustration would set in and he would threaten to give up because his playing was so inept. However, I urged him to go on practising: "Frustrations are part of creativity." I tell him that it is not just a way of passing the time, but an existentially significant form of self-expression. Via music, he found his way back to his adolescent self, with all the pain and elation that implied. During this stage, Wolf succeeded in squaring up to the challenges at work. Repeatedly, we contemplated ways in which he could organise his vocational routines and master difficult situations. He was surprised to find that after his return to work, he had been welcomed with a great deal of appreciation by his new team.

In the final stages of therapy, Wolf engages not only with love conflicts and job plans but also with spiritual themes. He has joined a mildly Buddhist group where he sings in the choir and occasionally meditates. He also attends Catholic and Protestant services. He finds the crucifixion theology of the Christian churches off-putting and is actively repelled by the brutality of the Old Testament. In the mornings, he walks along the river bank doing the Tai-Chi exercises I introduced him to at the outset of therapy: "There is something divine in breathing, movement, and nature."

In the final brief therapy session, Wolf sums up by saying that the treatment has put the ground back under his feet. This is because of the opportunity "just to talk" and in this way "to get closer to oneself". The rules imposing structure and rhythm on his everyday life have helped, plus the opportunity to get a clearer picture of himself. Here, however, "much still needs to be done". He still feels very unstable and believes that he has a lot of work ahead. But now, at least, he is "rooted" in his world again. He regards the suggestion to look on everyday existence as a creative task very important but, as that "doesn't happen from one day to the next", he would like to continue with psychotherapy. We agree on two sessions a week. He wants to try the couch, which he has been thinking about for some time: "Maybe it makes it easier to fantasise freely."

Although the serious initial lack of energy and the bouts of depression have clearly improved, Wolf is still in a state of unstable equilibrium. His subjacent despondency corresponds to the ambivalence in his personal relations. This makes itself felt after we have agreed on a continuation of therapy. Although he has succeeded in establishing a steady relationship with an obviously affectionate and loving female partner of his own age, he is repeatedly assailed by the urge to separate, an urge that he finds impossible to understand. In job terms, he has landed back on his feet, but he avoids any kind of contact with the "people at the top of the hierarchy" because they were the ones who treated him unfairly. This avoidance strategy leads to restrictions in his action radius and fruitless rumination. Sometimes, he is assailed by dropout impulses and wants to "throw it all in". He is uncertain about his role identity and feels reminded of his "wild years" when he turned away completely from his parents and the values they stood for. Up to now, he has been engaging with a mother he experienced as conventional and cold-hearted and an absentee father of an authoritarian cast of mind. Yet, both parents gave him plenty of opportunities, and the profession he opted for was the same as his father's.

As he gives himself over to this free play of ideas on the couch, new dimensions of his uncertain role identity come to the surface, together with emotional complications. Wolf begins to engage with the psychic traces left by his father's membership of the SS. After the collapse of the regime, his father "in his heart of hearts" had remained a convinced Nazi. Neither had his mother ever fully relinquished the values espoused by the Nazis. He had never been aware of this before, but now it gives him the "screaming abdabs" when he thinks of the world he grew up in. Suddenly, he can understand his teenage rebellion better. However, Wolf has difficulty appreciating that he, too, has a burden of guilt to face. He abandoned his Jewish wife and their two daughters when better opportunities presented themselves. He met her during his "dropout trip" to California. She came from a very difficult family background and had "worked her way up" with a great deal of tenacity. She always supported his vocational progress. After their separation, she was very badly off for a number of years and even today "she is not doing particularly well".

Wolf has "never genuinely" faced up to the significance of these events, let alone discussing them with anyone. Gradually, feelings of guilt at having left his wife come to the surface. Up to now, he had seen this as "merely a different course that one took". He remembers that when he first took his fiancée home to meet the family, his mother whispered to him, "Does she have to be Jewish?" Only now does he fully realise how terrible that was. Triggered by these memories, serious inner complications ensue. Wolf engages with his own mistakes and his subtly aggressive attitude. He senses that realistic guilt feelings are an important factor in getting to grips with the flaws in his behaviour and remedying them.

Wolf keeps returning to Germany's historical shame and guilt. He asks himself what it means to be part of a nation that has committed racist crimes. He concedes that he is not actively guilty of these crimes himself, but goes on to accuse himself of a degree of involvement because of the way he has profited from his parents' wealth: "How can you just go out and enjoy life with a burden like that?" A dream illustrates his quest for personal truth and pleasure in life:

> It was the last day before a trial in the USA in which I was to be accused of having run down and killed a child under the influence of alcohol. On this, my last day of freedom, the sky was radiantly blue and a huge, long beach tempted me to go for a swim. But I couldn't relish the swim because of the panic and fear weighing down on me. I knew I was guilty, but I was not sure how much evidence there was against me. I felt sure that among all the twisted bodies and car wrecks at the scene of the accident where I had run over the child they would find DNA traces that would betray me. I was expecting the death sentence. So far, I had simply denied everything, which enabled me to carry on working as usual in a public office. I wanted to enjoy the beach and the blue sky just one more time because I was convinced they were going to execute me.

After contemplating a large number of associations triggered by this dream, Wolf asks himself how the "strange entanglements" in his past and his ambivalence on so many issues will have affected his daughters. One of them is successful, a "cool company consultant" and very "straight", the other has "dropped out" of society, takes drugs, and rebels against any kind of structure. In their very different ways, they are both extremely "nice". Wolf sees them as representing the two sides of his personality that he has such difficulty in reconciling with one another. On the one hand, he sees himself as overadjusted; on the other, as a "rebel without a cause". This is why he has such trouble dealing with conflicts: "When the going gets hard, I don't have a clear standpoint." These fluctuations also make themselves felt in the therapeutic context. He needs a shoulder to lean on, but, at the same time, he seems determined to go his own way.

Wolf gives me the impression that he is capable of using the therapeutic setting (recumbent on the couch) as a transitional space helping him to "find his way back to himself" in a process of remembrance, repetition, and working through. He prefers me to limit my interpretations to a minimum, relishing the opportunity to talk about whatever occurs to him without anyone mapping out a route for him to follow. Occasionally, I feel superfluous and have to rein in my therapeutic commitment and my ideas. Ultimately, however, we find a way of harnessing our exchanges and drawing upon Wolf's images and dreams to get to grips with difficult emotions. Increasingly, Wolf is able to accept life as a creative task, not only in our sessions, but also in his everyday routines.

After three years of largely psychoanalytic therapy (two sessions a week, 240 all told), we were able to terminate the treatment. Wolf sums up. His situation has changed radically: "At the outset I was completely off the rails, submerged by a huge pile of crap. I was no longer capable of working or living, I was at the end of my tether." Now things are completely different: not only is he back on an even keel, he has learnt a great deal about himself and the world. In fact, he feels better now than he did before the job issues triggered the crisis.

In his view, a wide variety of things have been helpful. Initially it was mainly the regular sessions that gave him stability: "I could talk about absolutely anything like I could with no one else." The structure imposed on his everyday life was also very important: regular exercise, no alcohol, gradual return to work. But even more significant was the fact "that I could accept myself again". This, however, came to full fruition only in the psychoanalytic phase of treatment: "Facing up to my own biography was the most important thing." He has a clear conception of his conflicts; his entanglement with his parents' history, puberty, his friendships, love relationships, and sexuality all have greater definition than before. Getting to grips with these topics has triggered a process in which he has learnt to accept himself as normal. His feelings of guilt in connection with chaotic relationships have given way to realistic concerns: "I am no longer at loggerheads with myself and everyone else." Therapy was a transitional space in which he found his way back to himself.

Why could he not have achieved much the same results by talking to friends? He would never presume to "get on his friends' nerves" in this way for hours on end. Therapy was an opportunity to "go through everything in detail and set my own priorities". He never had the impression he was being criticised. Between the actual sessions, he still felt the presence of an inner partner desisting from blame or condemnation. In the sessions, the emphasis was always on positive responses and solutions: "That increased my mindfulness and my feeling of selfhood. In the last analysis, therapy meant accompanying me on the path to myself and to others." Before therapy, he had often "felt as if people were looking at him sideways. This feeling has now dissolved into thin air."

At our final meeting, I give Wolf a brief description of the ABCDE model and ask him to evaluate the individual dimensions. He gives a score of eight to the significance of active support and stabilisation (A). Advice on behavioural matters (B) was also very important, at least initially. He awards a score of seven for this. Less important in his eyes was the discussion of inappropriate thoughts, concepts, and attitudes (C). He gives this a three. Much more crucial was the perception of hitherto unconscious conflicts (D). This was achieved by immersing himself in his own biography as well as by discussing his present relational conflicts. Wolf gives this sector full marks (a ten). At some point, however, this preoccupation with his biography had outlived its value, and he felt "no inclination to talk about my granny for the hundredth time". Ultimately, it was the space he had to himself and in which, with my assistance, he was able to understand and accept himself (E) that rounded off the therapy successfully. To this existential dimension, Wolf also gives a score of ten.

His assessment largely agrees with mine. In terms of the integrative model, therapy commenced with stabilising interventions and the therapist's personally supportive attitude (A). On this basis, Wolf was able to accept behaviour-regulating suggestions (B) and correct negative views and attitudes (C). As early as at the brief therapy stage, biographically conditioned conflicts gained significance (D). With his narratives, fantasies, and dreams, he was able to mentalize emotionally significant relational experiences. He used the therapeutic exchanges to better understand himself and others and face up to the existential task of self-realisation (E). He sums the whole process up as follows: "I found myself again, in fact, maybe I discovered myself for the first time."

I asked Wolf for his consent to the publication of his case history. He agreed and said he would like to read what I had written about him. Naturally, I said this would be fine, but I had rather ambiguous feelings about the possible outcome and asked him if he wanted to discuss his assessment and criticism with me. He said yes he would, and we agreed to meet a week later. To my relief, he said he had read the report with pleasure and profit. He was grateful to have had the chance to go through it and see things from my perspective. He found it important and helpful, referring to it as the "finishing touch" to his therapy. He felt he had been understood "in his essentials". Wolf sees the discussion of my report as a significant part of the therapy and says he wants to pay for this session as well. I turn down his offer.

There were also a few things in my report that surprised him. He had completely forgotten his dreams and my interpretations of them. This does not, however, mean that they were unimportant. I am reminded of the image of dreams and fantasies surfacing from the unconscious like flying fish, revealing themselves briefly and then returning to swim on in the unconscious. Wolf finds it very important that therapists should preserve the things said in the course of the sessions. The best thing, however, was "to be whole, or, rather, to learn to live the way one really is".

Psychotic episodes: a musician seeks ecstasy and ends in chaos

"How can I find my way between fascinating thrills and dreadful horrors?"

After a long plane flight followed by a "psychedelic" party with unlimited amounts of alcohol, Berthold, a twenty-five-year-old musician, "freaked out with a vengeance". He had to undergo a five-month course of treatment at a psychiatric hospital far away from his home. Although this therapy helped him, he is determined never to experience another "horror trip" like this one. At the hospital, he was soon able to calm down, but his inner isolation scared him. The medication made him feel "woozy" and he found the diagnosis, "schizophrenia", frightening in the extreme. He does not want to go through such horrors again. He had previously gone in search of psychotherapeutic treatment but terminated a brief course of therapy because his (female) therapist made sexual advances to him.

Berthold makes a timid and desperate impression. At the same time, he comes across as rather contemptuous and patronising. However, I have a good feeling about the connection between us, and we are soon operating in a trustful atmosphere. Initially, of course, the deeper roots from which this understanding relationship springs remain unconscious. Berthold is obviously looking for someone to stabilise and guide him. He expects me to help him get on top of his mood swings and avoid chaotic states. At the same time, he senses that it is up to him to change his behaviour. He also wants to understand his feelings better. While I naturally intend to honour my professional obligations, I know that this will only be possible with empathy and understanding. I also see it as a challenge to accompany him on his path to creative self-realisation.

In our therapeutic efforts immediately after hospitalisation, we first attempt to stabilise his life-style. I am surprised to see how readily this young man, whose major concern is obviously to flout as many of the limits imposed on him as he can, is prepared to accept quite simple suggestions designed to give structure to his everyday life. We agree on well-defined routines and are both surprised to see how much this does to establish a protective equilibrium: regular working hours, a half-hour run at noon, reading with soft background music in the evening. After a few sessions, Berthold tells me that although he did not initially find these suggestions very convincing, they do, in fact, help him "not to boil over". We also invest some time in rectifying inappropriate convictions.

For a long time, Berthold had felt that a creative artist had to be a bit "off-centre". But even in early youth he found that the effect that hashish had on him was more soporific than anything else. Yet, he still took this drug for a lengthy period because it made him feel "different". He wanted to transcend "the narrow limits of daily life". At parties, he was often able to "beam himself away" with large amounts of alcohol. Yet, deep down, he has long been clear in his mind that he can only work "as an artist" when he is "stone-cold sober". He had steered clear of "hard drugs" after witnessing the harm they did to friends and acquaintances.

When he is able to discipline himself, he composes small piano pieces that also find favour at the music academy. But, for his taste, the work phases are too short. He has difficulty in summoning up the patience required to realise his plans, but he has seen and learnt enough to resist the temptation to wallow in cannabis instead of working. He realises how important discipline and well-defined structures are for his work. As Nietzsche once noted, "One must have some chaos left inside to give birth to a dancing star." But how much chaos is productive, and when does it turn into barren confusion? Berthold learns to be more conscious in managing the balance between order, without which he cannot work, and chaos, without which nothing occurs to him.

In family matters, things are invariably "high-octane". Sometimes, he feels depressed, at other times confused; frequently he just "scrams". Given that he is just out of hospital, I advise him to avoid exchanges that are likely to get him worked up. In the therapeutic sessions, he makes use of the free space available to him to work out for himself "what is actually going on" between the members of his family. We also try to cast light on other relationships, notably with women, that regularly knock him off balance. While he longs for a love relationship, he also fears anyone getting too close. During treatment, he falls in love with a young woman who lives a long way away. But passionate encounters quickly overtax him, and he fears losing control: "When I get close to a woman, I can't feel myself any more. My thoughts start spinning, I can't rein them in." Accordingly, we devise more everyday rituals designed to avoid confusing situations. Together, we go through his relationships so as to better understand his vulnerability. We elaborate behaviours that will help him protect himself against hazardous experiences. He has mixed feelings about the medication I have prescribed for him. He finds that while it does indeed shield him from unpleasant occurrences, it also numbs his responses. Against the professional guidelines, we start reducing the high-potency neuroleptics after a few weeks, as he is no longer able to stand the way they daze him and rob him of his energy.

This is the time at which we begin investigating his biography more closely. His mother was an ambitious physician with high aims in life. Her pregnancy with Berthold was a high-risk affair; after his birth she suffered from depression for a number of years. In fact, she never fully recovered. She is still resentful of the fact that she could not have the professional career she had mapped out for herself. Berthold's father is a musician who has always kept family complications at arm's length despite his devotion to the individual members. In Berthold's descriptions, he remains an oddly nebulous figure. The image of an engulfing mother and encroaching siblings dominates Berthold's view of things. In his earliest memories "everything is somehow uncanny". The first experience he can remember took place sometime between his second and third birthday. He climbed out of his cot to join his twin sister in hers. In so doing, he fell and broke his arm. Ever since he was five, he would hold his sister's hand after they had been read a goodnight story. As they fell asleep, they would imagine what it would be like to be dead. Frequently, they contemplated lying down on the nearby railway tracks.

In puberty, he became aware that he was unable to feel pleasure: "I was always despondent, but I didn't know what was getting me down." He was usually able to play down these moods, but sometimes they were so distressing that he contemplated suicide. Neither could he always control his aggressive urges. This led to the termination of friendships and trouble with his teachers: "I was a really naughty boy, the teachers were furious with me." Because he regularly smoked hashish between sixteen and eighteen, he lost a lot of weight and his pallor was extreme. His fellow students gave him the nickname "Death". He has no idea why he harmed himself in this way and could be so unpleasant to others. He is equally unable to understand why he would sometimes upset his girlfriends with his cynicism and arrogance, even though he was in love with them. The slightest incident was enough to make him feel injured and insulted.

At university, Berthold was greatly respected. Many of his professors did what they could to support him, and he was greatly motivated by acceptance into a foundation for the unusually gifted. At the same time, he had a guilty conscience because he felt he did not deserve such favour. He opted for therapy after his twin sister had tried to kill herself and was only rescued at the last minute.

After the first few weeks of treatment, in which we concentrated on measures designed to regulate his behaviour, Berthold's narcissistic conflicts began to clamour for attention. He remembers how he had resorted to drugs to sort out his lack of self-worth. Repelled by the "boring attachments" to his parents and his relations with "idiotic friends", he found that everything "made him puke" and decided to "moss off somewhere else". He has a dream connected with this topic:

I'm in a shopping centre, everything glitters and belongs to me. An alluring woman appears and smiles at me enticingly. She offers me a drug and her eyes keep me under her spell. I am fascinated and aroused. Then I find myself in a maze. Everything turns garish and confusing, I don't know where I am and start losing my mind. When I wake up, I look round at my room and think how humdrum it all is.

In connection with the dream, Berthold tells me that he frequently experiences everyday life as boring. We discover that he can transcend his boundaries with the help of alluring fantasies. But this involves the risk of losing control over his feelings and ideas. Creativity is not only the discovery of novelty and fascination, but also the selection of the things I can use and the patience to work on them.

After a few weeks, he tells me about another dream:

> It is wartime and I'm smoking pot with a friend. We have no idea what's going on until I get scared and go looking for my family. They are all lying in one big bed, parents and siblings, and awkwardly trying to hide themselves. I need to do something to somehow make sure they survive.

Berthold sees the dream as an expression of his inner chaos, which stops him from taking an interest in others. He senses the way in which he extinguishes embarrassing memories of important persons. But this also deprives him of his internal companions. The repression of feelings, thoughts, and relational experiences leaves him with feelings of guilt. These can be so torturous that he splits them off and seeks better feelings by indulging in drink. Berthold's dreams put him in touch with important feelings and split-off experiences. He sees them as an expression of those experiences and arrives at insightful conclusions that would otherwise have been inaccessible. "Dreams are interesting commentaries on me and my relationships," he says.

He is glad that therapy is helping him to get a better grip on life. Another dream:

> I'm a student attending various seminars. In the lecture hall, I have a little dragon in my hand with wings and a long tail. It gets bigger and bigger but I can still control it.

This dream addresses his longing to achieve something great without being destroyed in the process. At the same time, sexual topics take centre stage. Here, again, ideas of grandeur rub shoulders with feelings of inferiority. As he engages with his sexuality, he falls in love with a girl student in the same year as he is.

After six months of treatment, Berthold can devote himself unreservedly to his studies. He can accept the well-defined work structures I proposed to him and senses that he needs this "scaffolding".

He no longer requires the high-strength neuroleptic drugs he has been taking. To "be on the safe side", he goes on taking a small dose of a low-potency neuroleptic. He is glad to have an improved feeling for his body, to no longer feel so immured and to start reducing the weight he put on as a result of the medication: "I felt as if I was disabled." He hopes that, in artistic terms, things will now develop further and has a dream:

> In my room there are eggs that have been laid by exotic birds. Somehow it's my job to hatch them. At first I don't want to, but then I take the time needed— the process is both boring and troublesome—and in the end a lovely bird comes out of the egg.

However, such graphic dreams are very much the exception in the otherwise tedious psychotherapeutic progress we are making. It is a tough task to transform Berthold's narcissistic ideas of grandeur into concrete artistic work. At least he now plays the piano regularly, which improves his feeling of coherence and boosts his self-confidence.

His thoughts are increasingly focused on his relationships with women. He has no difficulty making contact but quickly loses interest, especially once he has slept with the woman in question. By contrast, he spends three months pursuing a twenty-two-year-old who refuses to "go all the way". Finally, she gives in and after that loses all her attraction for him. He himself finds this impossible to understand because she is tender and loving. He feels as if he is losing himself in her and also losing contact with his own body. In this connection, Berthold gives me a drawing he did when he was four years old. It shows a huge woman clad in light-blue slacks and a shriekingly red pullover reaching out to grab a very small boy. He considers the drawing an accurate representation of the relationship between his mother and himself. A green balloon emerging from his mouth contains the word "Mama" and appears to fade away unheard. In the upper left-hand corner is a small bird with a sharp beak looking beadily at the woman.

Berthold feels that this picture perfectly illustrates his absolute helplessness *vis-à-vis* his mother. In it, she appears overpowering and impulse-driven. He sees the cheeky little bird as an aspect of his own self. It is free and untrammelled and can defend itself with its sharp beak. Berthold sees a link between this symbolisation of the relationship with his mother and his present dilemma: "When a woman opens her arms to me, she becomes overpowering. I know it's ridiculous, but I really am afraid of being devoured." Perhaps this is why he has to keep loving women at arm's length with "snide" remarks. In his fear of powerful women—"and a woman in love is always powerful"—he repeatedly has visions of his mother, to whom his father "was inferior on all counts". At this point, Berthold tells me of a recurrent sexual fantasy in which he and a friend have "fizzing sex" with a woman. The image that presents itself to me is that Berthold is looking for a male companion to protect him from being consumed by the females of the species. Conceivably, this fear of women might also be fuelled by the fear of losing his inner order and structure in arousing situations. His friend (or his therapist) would then be a protective companion helping him to assert himself in the face of confusing passions.

At this stage of treatment, he recalls another dream:

My girlfriend approaches my bed. I feel aroused and confused. Then I'm flying into the recesses of a wide-open vagina. It's like being born, but the other way round.

Perhaps his longing for closeness is so intense that he actually wants to lose himself and be devoured and his occasionally brusque and offensive responses are a way of warding off such wishes. He remembers a playmate he was basically very fond of but whom he persuaded to grasp an open razor blade with his bare hand. Afterwards, he was "awfully shocked" by what he had done. After his sister's attempted suicide, his feelings of guilt were so powerful that he felt like a Nazi war criminal.

Berthold gradually realises that in some hard-to-fathom way there is a connection between his aggressive impulses and guilt feelings on the one hand, and his ideas of grandeur and his fantasies about being infinitely small on the other. He is glad to be able to perceive and work on this in therapy. In this connection, he comes back to his childhood drawing: "My mother is so overpowering. But the aggressive little bird is independent and free." He sees the bird as a symbol of his sexuality, which he is increasingly able to enjoy. In this context, he tells me about a game called "The Birds' Wedding" that he has been playing with fellow students. The participants put masks on and then take all their clothes off. He finds this very arousing and is fascinated to see how freed one can be just by wearing a mask.

Given his efforts to achieve independence and sexual freedom, it is surprising that Berthold's guilt feelings *vis-à-vis* his mother are still so pronounced. He discovers a heartfelt desire to make his mother happy. In his dealings with women, he is still liable to "blow hot and cold", veering between keen interest and aloof withdrawal. This is also perceptible in his relationship with me. Berthold can be very winning and then suddenly give me the cold shoulder for no apparent reason. Sometimes, he behaves like a personal friend or even an admirer, only to withdraw into his shell without warning.

Therapy focuses on these topics for several months. Initially, behavioural strategies had been the main concern, but now the time has come to work on Berthold's psychic conflicts. He finds the opportunity to spend three hours a week on the couch talking freely about his thoughts and feelings liberating in the extreme. He can review his biography in close-up and compares the situation with writing a novel: "You find yourself." He produces dreams that "explain his life" for him. Engagement with ideas of grandeur and fantasies of infinite smallness makes his self-image more realistic. He also learns to better understand the feelings of others.

After about eighteen months of treatment, Berthold begins to engage with transgenerational conflicts. His grandfather profited from the war and remained a convinced Nazi even after the downfall of the Reich. His children, "all left-wing, of course", still live off the money he left them. His father never worked and invariably played the role of understanding bohemian. For the family, he never really existed. No one knew what he got up to all day. There are many secrets in the family, lots of "emotional undergrowth". It took some time to prune that undergrowth in therapy.

In "pruning the undergrowth", Berthold's feelings of guilt *vis-à-vis* his sister play a central role. He himself is esteemed by his professors and now has a number of good friends. By contrast, his twin sister has trouble coping with her studies and lives a very withdrawn life: "At birth I was the stronger one and pushed her out of the way." In puberty, on the other hand, he had felt cornered and encroached on by her. Once he cut her likeness out of a family photo and threw it angrily into the refuse bin. But when she held out her hand to him in hospital after her attempted suicide, he was invaded by a feeling reminiscent of those that prompted him to scale his sister's cot. They are very close, but they are also very aware of the destructive forces that threaten to drive them apart.

After two years of therapy, Berthold does his degree as a music teacher and is sent to a fairly distant town for his period of probationary teaching. Initially, we phone once a week. He is grateful for this support, not least because he is having problems with his female colleagues. His supervisor has openly propositioned him, and one of the other women is jealous: "Rival mares lashing out at each other, and me the poor little bird stuck in the middle." He finds it helpful to talk to me and to defend himself against encroachments. He finished his probationary period with excellent grades and now works on a half-day basis and starts a jazz formation. He consults me once or twice a year "when there's something special to talk about".

At our last session, I ask Berthold to give me his views on the course taken by his therapy. First he talks about the helpful things: "Your presence gave me security. You were always there. Your advice about achieving greater discipline during the working day and in leisure time was not always easy to act upon but it was very helpful. The most important thing was that I could talk and paint a picture of my life. Today, I have a better understanding of my feelings and relationships. In the last resort, you supported me in discovering my music."

Three years after the termination of therapy, I ask Berthold's permission to publish a report on his treatment in an anonymous form. He has no objections: "You did something for me as well." But he wants to read what I have to say before it is published. I agree and he sends me a number of corrections. He feels, however, that the description is accurate and the summary realistic. I give him a brief explanation of the ABCDE model and ask him to evaluate the different levels. He says that the stabilising and supportive aspects of the therapeutic relationship (A) were important and awards this side of therapy seven. Equally important were the behavioural dimensions (B). Learning to impose structure and rhythm on his everyday life has lost none of its significance. Well-defined organisation of work and leisure stabilises him and it is important to practise systematic self-management. Accordingly, he gives this segment of the model a score of seven. Imposing (corrective) order on opinions and prejudices (C) was significant. This still helps him when he is in danger of floundering in the classroom. Problems are easier to deal with when he consciously thinks through the situation in question and contemplates it from different angles. He feels that this approach also goes down well with his students. The more perspectives he has at his disposal, the better the work produced by the class: "As in therapy, intellectual understanding is very good for the relationship." Accordingly, he also gives the cognitive side of therapy a score of seven.

The psychodynamic elements (D) he finds less easy to relate to because many things that surfaced from the unconscious sank back down there shortly afterwards. However, it was still important to work on his biography in order to better perceive and understand his present conflicts. Dreams and free-floating ideas helped to improve his sensitivity for his feelings and achieve a better understanding of his relationships. His relationship to me was also significant, but it was difficult for him to say why or how. Altogether he gives the psychodynamic–psychoanalytic dimension a score between six and eight. He emphasises, however, that the importance of this dimension fluctuated greatly in the course of therapy. Initially, the main thing was stabilisation via behavioural strategies, followed by cognitive elements. After that stage, the process plumbed profounder depths and the psychoanalytic dimensions came to the fore. The fundamental point was the opportunity to talk about himself in the presence of an understanding listener. This made it easier for him to get nearer to his own self and accept it for what it was. The existential plane (E), which he used to verbalise diffuse moods and confusing thoughts, he gives a score of seven , emphasising that this aspect was closely associated with the first.

Looking back on the medication, Berthold says that at the outset it had indeed helped to allay his confusion. The tablets had a calming effect on him. Soon, however, this was supplanted by the feeling of being controlled from the outside. He no longer knew whether this was part of his disorder or an effect of the tablets. After five months in hospital, he also felt that the medication was slowing him down and numbing his perceptions. Only after a progressive reduction of the doses was he able to read and learn again. He sees the reduction of medication three months after hospital and total discontinuation after six months as a result of frequent and regular psychotherapy:

"I wouldn't have managed it with appointments only every two or four weeks. I am totally convinced that if I had gone on taking high-dosage medication for much longer, I would never have finished my studies and held my own in the probationary teaching stint."

Borderline personality traits: long-term psychotherapy helps to understand feelings and relationships

"I can't control myself and I'm afraid of bursting open"

The patient in this last of my narratives in this book is someone I have known for thirty years. Mara was the first person with whom I embarked on a course of psychotherapy after finishing my training. I was in charge of a student counselling centre, and counselling and brief therapy was all I was called upon to perform. Outside my regular job, it was also the first time that I had had a chance to embark on long-term psychotherapy where I saw fit to do so. Mara phoned to ask for an appointment as soon as possible: "I can't control my feelings any more and I'm afraid of bursting open. If this goes on, I really can't say where it might lead . . ."

With these descriptions in mind, I was taken aback by Mara's independent and laid-back attitude at the first interview: "I don't really need anyone." She tells me that alongside studying to be a teacher, she was an active party member and supported the women's rights movement. The thing is that she is always quarrelling with her (women) friends and ultimately feels unable to establish any lasting relationships. She has been for therapy before but her therapist fell ill and had to break up therapy. As a small child, the impression she had of her mother was of someone unapproachable and constantly overtaxed. Physically, she found her mother unappealing and "somehow repulsive". Things were easier with her father. For a long time, she was his favourite child and she could talk to him about anything and everything. Accordingly, she has no trouble holding constructive conversations with male intellectuals: "But if they get too close, I start panicking." Brief sexual encounters were "brill" but afterwards she felt "like a puddle of vomit": "I can't stand closeness."

For all her sophistication and apparent self-possession, the first sessions reveal major insecurity and diffuse anxiety behind the laidback façade. After three sessions, she "confesses", "There are moments when the ground beneath my feet just falls away. Sometimes I'm so confused that I feel like jumping out of the window." She contemplates throwing herself in front of a train, as one of her girlfriends did. These announcements make me feel very unsure of myself. Before Mara's arrival, I had been looking forward to some serious, independent psychotherapy at last, but now I am faced with a dangerous situation. I seek advice from one of my former supervisor, who encourages me not to have Mara hospitalised but to stay in the outpatient sector with her: "If you can accept the patient and not let yourself be confused, you should square up to the challenge. And always stay free and responsive!"

Mara assures me that as long as she is undergoing treatment, she will not do herself any harm. I sense a reliable bond between us. Contrary to my normal principle of restricting brief therapy to one session a week, I offer Mara four hours, which she accepts with obvious relief. Without frequent contact, she would be unable to withstand the pressure.

In previous years, she had already undergone behavioural and psychodynamic therapy. Behavioural therapy she found helpful for only a short time. The explanations and good advice she received had no lasting effect and did nothing to impose order on her emotional chaos. She found her therapist (a woman) pleasant and competent, but "It just wasn't right for me." Psychodynamic therapy with one session every two weeks was also insufficient for her needs. The insights she developed were interesting, but contact was not frequent enough. In Mara's view, this therapist (again a woman) had trouble focusing on her because she had just lost her mother.

The first few sessions with Mara are difficult. She describes her "emotional chaos" but I find it hard to understand what she is saying. She tells me about the girlfriend who threw herself in front of a train. It is an event that she keeps coming back to. She asks herself whether she might not be better off in a psychiatric hospital. She suspects that medication will not be sufficient to lighten the chaos she is suffering from: "I must get the better of it myself." After a while, Mara begins to find the frequent sessions reassuring. She feels less confused and finds it easier to talk about herself and her life. In her case, the couch position supports her efforts to impose order on her emotional and intellectual chaos. Mara tells me that in the recumbent position she finds it easier to follow up her ideas than in a sedentary, face-to-face arrangement. The regular appointments and my reliable presence do her good, she says. On the other hand, she is disparaging about the chosen setting. "Psychoanalysis is old hat!" she says. "All this poring over feelings, dreams, and ideas. You have to go out and do something!"

In the first weeks of treatment, she alternates between testy accusations and an abject fear that I might decide not to expose myself to her verbal assaults any longer. She repeatedly dwells on the idea that I might fall seriously ill or even die. My initial impressions are fragmentary. I find no internal images that might help me understand Mara's plight. Frequently, I catch myself not listening properly and find it difficult to recall much of what she has said. Nothing occurs to me in response to her dreams and ideas. Contact is usually extremely tiring, but at least it is stable.

After three months, there is a two-week hiatus in the sessions due to my vacation. At the first session after my holiday Mara is extremely bad-tempered: "In both those weeks I was completely paralysed by despair. Sometimes I felt as if I were dead." Shortly before my return, she started feeling "completely confused and possessed by a mysterious, ungovernable rage." She asks whether it might not be better to discontinue the therapy. The tone of Mara's voice is enraged; she conveys a diffuse impression of anxiety, alarm, and rejection. Doubts assail me as to whether psychoanalytic therapy really is right for her. Suddenly, images of actual abortions impinge on my inward eye. Although there has been no reference to this in what my patient has told me, I find myself engaging with child murders.

As I focus on my fantasies and on painful memories of unpleasant things that have happened to me, my confusion begins to recede. After some brief reflection on these graphic imaginings in which I attempt to distinguish my own conflicts from those of the patient, it occurs to me that the separation caused by my vacation might have revived an abortion trauma in Mara. True, Mara had frequently contrived to achieve a kind of self-creation with her intellectualism. But now she seems to be feeling a longing for a reliable attachment. She suspects that she may be yearning for a relationship that is fruitful for both parties. I make reference to this longing and then suggest, "Perhaps your longing is so intense that even slight setbacks disappoint and annoy you out of all proportion. You get so mad that you even start attacking what is creative in our relationship. Maybe your disappointment with me has prompted you to destroy what has been taking shape between us, our joint work."

After a brief silence, Mara tells me reflectively that she has just been visited by a very graphic image: "A baby was being slaughtered just above my head. It was terrible, monstrous." My attitude encourages her to follow up this image. She realises how much she longs for a stable relationship: "This chaotic rage of mine probably ruins everything." After a while I say, "Perhaps you have such an urgent need to protect your reference persons, including me, that you have to get rid of yourself in time. That, of course, means attacking what is growing in you." Mara is silent for a while, then says that she feels an urgent desire to share things with me: "The partition between us has fallen away." She recalls a harrowing scene from her childhood but is uncertain whether this is a genuine memory or a fantasy taking its cue from things her parents told her. As a small child she was very weak. No one ever found out why.

When she was one going on two, she was hospitalised and her death seemed unavoidable. Her parents were not allowed to get anywhere near her and could only wave from outside. She remembers now that when she was discharged, her father was the only one she re-established contact with. Her mother appeared to be a complete stranger to her; she no longer wanted anything to do with her. Mara connects this memory with her separation anguish, the kind of anguish she went through in my case as well. She reacts to this anguish with rage and does everything she can to extinguish even the good things in a relationship. The tendency to break off a relationship when it starts posing problems is something she is familiar with from her working life. In the therapy situation, she has repeated this tendency. Now she understands why, in relationships, she is always so ready to damn everything into the ground as soon as the going gets a little harder. She sees herself threatening to forfeit my attention in the same way as she spurned her mother's affections after her spell in hospital.

A positive experience for Mara is that when problems crop up, we do not simply go our different ways but stay together and do our best to understand her rage impulses. She notes with some satisfaction that this is helping her impose a little more order on her emotional chaos. Something similar is happening on my side as well. Mara triggers feelings in me that I sometimes find confusing. But she also enables me to generate graphic fantasies that help give some kind of form to otherwise disorderly arousals. I find this similar to an artistic process in which chaotic urges and impulses are organised aesthetically.

In the case we are talking about, this kind of thing also happens tacitly. As an example, we can look at the way a symptom develops. Up to the onset of psychotherapy, Mara had suffered from bouts of asthma that required medical treatment. After a few weeks, she left her anti-asthma spray in my office; her breathing troubles had disappeared into thin air. Obviously, Mara was able to use the treatment situation as a play-space in which she could shape her conflicts creatively. This might well be what made concretisation in the form of a psychosomatic symptom superfluous. Only two years later, when Mara became pregnant and started engaging with her own motherhood, did she recall that at the age of eight to ten she would climb into her mother's bed every night. This made the nocturnal bouts of asthma go away. She was using psychotherapy in a similar way. It was a protective transitional space where Mara could enact her psychic drama. The roles she allotted to me in this process were very wide-ranging: supportive reference person who did not withdraw from conflicts; understanding interlocutor; amanuensis helping to write the story of her life.

Much of the attachment between us was, of course, unconscious. The course of treatment lasted almost three years. Mara terminated her therapy when she met and fell in love with a man and moved away to a distant city with him. She felt sure that her academic credentials would get her a good job there.

Ten years after the termination of therapy, which I described in a scientific paper (2003), Mara gets in touch with me again. Her two sons are doing well; sometimes she asks herself how she could be so "intact". Her marriage to a writer, suffering at this moment in time from writer's block, is very satisfactory. She has carved out a career for herself as a teacher and is proud of being "respected for what I do". Accordingly, she cannot fathom why she should, on occasion, suffer from attacks of groundless despondency and inner paralysis. Frequently, she accuses herself of being a "bitch" because, although her marriage is happy, she repeatedly indulges in extramarital affairs: "I know exactly how self-destructive that is, and it's also harmful for my children, but . . ." She wants to resume psychotherapy but can only manage one session a week because of the long distances involved.

Right at the beginning of our first session I am assailed by ill-defined anxiety and disquiet, surprising though this in the face of Mara's sophisticated and self-possessed behaviour. She tells me how glad she is that she can come back to me. Psychoanalysis had been an entirely good thing for her, although all her colleagues speak disparagingly of it. Her sons are very important to her: "The fact that they're doing so well shows me that I can't be as bad as I sometimes think." She is concerned about a trainee teacher whom she has been looking after. Their contact has become very personal and the young woman reveals secret matters to her that she does not tell anyone else about. Mara's professional counselling and supervision is good, but the personal relationship is beginning to confuse her.

The content of what she confides in me is basically harmless, and yet, as things go on, I feel a degree of alarm. I put some careful questions to her. She tells me quite readily that her trainee is very lonely, smokes far too much, and has little idea of what to do with herself. During my patient's account, I think of my own lonely days as a child. One image that presents itself to me is of myself playing on the slippery banks of a raging river. How easily I might have fallen in and drowned! This reminds me for the first time that in her earlier analysis Mara was intensely preoccupied by the subject of a lost or dying child. I ask her whether she has ever encountered anything stunted, lifeless, or disturbing in her young trainee. The graphic image that presents itself to Mara in response is that of her mother: "Why did my mother take so little notice of me . . . Probably she was too exhausted to do so . . . Mother looks sad and has no place for me . . . I am like a foreign body inside her . . . She must get rid of me." After Mara has dwelt on these images and memories for some time, she appears relieved, as if an oppressive veil had been lifted. I, too, feel relieved of my paralysing inertia, as if life had at least partially been restored. But then images of dismembered children come to mind and I find myself thinking of possible abortion attempts by my patient's parents.

At the start of the next session, the patient says once again how much good it does her to come and see me. With a degree of unease, I see the image of an intimate but lifeless couple before me. My patient tells me that although they were unhappy, her parents had decided to stick it out together. As I listen, the image of "deadly" boredom comes to mind, which Mara had referred to earlier as typical of life in her parents' house: the mother depressive, absent, lifeless, the father compulsively steeped in his own activities. After experiencing this for a while, my chest feels constricted and I am visited by something that feels like a "sickness unto death", a strange gravitation towards chaos and death.

Then I think of my own attempts to rebel against anything and everything in puberty, the liberating feelings associated with the first sexual encounters. This puts me in touch with difficult experiences I have been through, the necessity to face up to relational conflicts if anything like a close relationship is to ensue. I interpret Mara's propensity for sexual adventures as a flight from closeness and constancy. Long-term attachments are bound up for her with father and mother and her fear of boredom and death. Her spontaneous response is to tell me that in the past few weeks she has repeatedly thought intensely about dying. She finds this very strange because she is happy with her husband, her children, and her job.

In the following sessions, the patient sets off on a journey into the past. She thinks of the abortion attempts undertaken by her mother, her own life-threatening illness when she was almost two, the unlived parts of her mother's personality, her father's loneliness. She frequently feels guilty about making unconscionable demands on me and ruining my health. She says that perhaps the most important thing about therapy was the way I always welcomed her back and "gave chaos a name". She asks herself whether one needs a whole life "to put the fragments together". After twenty-five sessions, Mara feels confident that she can carry on alone without my assistance.

Over twenty-five years after our first contact, we run into one another at a concert. Mara approaches me without hesitation and is very friendly: "I'm doing very well, although things are a little difficult at the moment. My sons are leaving home, going off to study at universities a long way away. Always these separations . . ." She still gets on very well with her husband. Some years ago, she found an elderly mentor who supports her in her job and always has time for her when problems crop up.

I ask Mara to answer a few questions I have in connection with her therapy. "Yes, of course," she says. Asked how she feels today in comparison to when she embarked on therapy, she says, "On a scale from nought to ten, two at the time and eight today." What does she think helped? I list the five factors in the ABCDE model for her to choose from. She gives the significance of the overall therapeutic relationship (A) a score of five. She rates the importance of behavioural interventions (B) at two. In her course of therapy, she also finds the intellectual correction of inappropriate attitudes (C) to be of minor importance and also gives this aspect of the treatment a score of two. There are various possible explanations for these low ratings. First, Mara had already been through a course of cognitive–behavioural therapy and was looking for alternative ways of dealing with her psychic problems. Second, she had encountered a very restricted form of behavioural therapy that took little account of her feelings. Third, her understanding of the cognitive dimension was a strictly manual-guided procedure that, in my experience, is hardly ever practised as rigidly as in her case. Hence, her unappreciative attitude to this kind of therapy. But probably the main reason for her aversion was that she "simply did not get on" with her therapist and for that reason rejected the method she was using.

In her eyes, insight into unconscious conflicts (D) was a very important part of her treatment. Mara gives this aspect a score of eight: "I learnt how to understand my unconscious affects and relational conflicts." The most important thing, however, was the opportunity to work through existential topics: attachment and passion, autonomy and dependency, duty and freedom. "It wasn't just waffle," she says, "I could take a close look at it and live through it all again. I could share everything with you. That was made a development possible that I would never have achieved otherwise." Accordingly, Mara gives the existential dimension of understanding (E) a score of ten.

Conclusion: an integrative ABCDE model of psychotherapy

Myths, religions, and philosophies contain any number of narratives that tell us how we can prevent or treat psychic disorders. Buddha, Confucius, Lao-tzu, Socrates, and Plato are illustrations of the fact that, in all high cultures, wise individuals have accompanied the depressed and confused on the path towards understanding their own feelings, ordering their thoughts, and giving their lives a meaningful shape. Cultural techniques with a psychotherapeutic impact figure very early on in the history of ideas. Physicians in ancient Greece acted in accordance with psychotherapeutic principles that sound astonishingly modern. They advocate (a) ongoing personal counselling from expert individuals, (b) health-supportive behaviour, (c) striving for clarity of mind, and (d) emotional equilibrium, plus (e) acceptance that life is a creative challenge.

These culturally ingrained therapeutic principles turn up over and over again in different guises and new degrees of sophistication. Unlike shamans, traditional and progressive psychotherapists do not recite magic spells or indulge in mumbo-jumbo. Their approach is rational and hard-headed. They treat psychic disorders on the basis of scientific principles and provide their patients with professional support as they set out on their quest for a healthy lifestyle, self-realisation, and social fulfilment. Many of them employ what is known as a "maieutic" approach (from the Greek word for midwife) and "deliver" their patients of the potential slumbering within.

Modern treatment techniques develop this traditional cultural practice further and attempt to substantiate it in scientific terms. New (or apparently new) techniques are "invented" at regular intervals. To achieve acceptance as scientific, they have no choice but to neglect cultural diversity and individual particularities. For science, the reduction of diversity and abstraction from individuality are defining criteria. However, therapeutic practice frequently obeys very different principles from scientific abstraction. Many psychotherapy researchers are alive to the problem. Back in the 1960s, Lazarus (1981) called for "technical eclecticism". Although many practitioners agreed with his views, the term "eclecticism" remained faintly reprehensible. It is often misunderstood as meaning a confused and confusing medley of different influences rather than the positive integration or marriage of elements that derive from different schools of thought and have proved their value in practice.

Another prominent psychotherapy researcher who called for the integration of different methods is Jerome Frank. In *Persuasion and Healing* (1991), the conclusion he draws from decades of research and therapeutic practice is that psychotherapy should be understood as the complex art of verbal exchange and understanding. Whether individual therapists relish the idea or not, it lies in the nature of human encounter that scientific assumptions and technical rules are embedded in practical communication. From the vantage point of philosophical anthropology, Gadamer (1976) and Ricoeur (1981) argue cogently that the theoretical sciences cannot develop rules for their practical application from within themselves. In psychotherapeutic practice, the meaningful and sensible application of rules is invariably an intersubjective and narrative process of mutual understanding.

The fact that it is only after many years of research that psychotherapists come up with ideas that extend existing theories and integrate them into complex models can be explained through research on memory and creativity. It is by no means unusual for supreme mathematical achievements to be performed by twenty-year-olds. Here, the importance of knowledge drawn from experience is less marked than in other fields. Scientists working on a closely defined and circumscribed problem may also reach the height of their powers at an early stage in their careers. There are many examples of Nobel Prize laureates in the sciences who were hardly older than thirty-five when they came up with the flash of genius that earned them the Prize. In the fields of high culture, politics, and philosophy, by contrast, complexity can frequently be managed only with advanced age (Holm-Hadulla, 2011).

Of course, psychotherapy is a highly complex field requiring a great deal of experiential knowledge. The generic model proposed by Orlinsky and Howard (1987) is exemplary in its description of the complexity of psychotherapeutic processes. Feixas and Botella (2004) approach integrative psychotherapy from a constructivist vantage point, while Wampold (2007) integrates individual techniques into a humanistic model of human relationships. The time has surely come for us to devise a way of unifying the complexity of psychotherapeutic encounter with individual technical elements and, thus, arriving at a holistic design. Our practical and integrative model is an attempt to reunify different techniques that have been artificially torn asunder.

While, on the face of it, the integration of psychotherapeutic methods seems a plausible proposition, it remains difficult to free oneself from the restrictions of one's own psychotherapeutic training. It is readily understandable that beginners venturing out into the complex field of psychotherapy should look for clear, scientifically substantiated rules on how to proceed. Those active in professional organisations also require hard-and-fast regulations and guidelines. Sound training in recognised therapeutic procedures is necessary and takes time, but the integration of different approaches could indeed take place earlier than is the case at the moment. Academic and, above all, professional resistance can be overcome. Professional representatives sense very quickly that they will lose touch with the therapists they are supposed to be representing if they shut themselves off from creative change. Scientific canons and institutional regulations will become sterile and bloodless if they ignore the particularities of therapeutic practice. Many aspects of human encounter cannot be explained objectively. They require a joint process of understanding. This is why individual experience is such a cardinal factor in psychotherapy.

For these reasons, I have derived fundamental principles from psychotherapeutic practice and described them with reference to actual cases. The principles I believe to be effective can be brought together in an integrative model:

A: creating a productive therapeutic relationship (Alliance);
B: modifying dysfunctional behaviour (Behaviour);
C: changing dysfunctional attitudes and beliefs (Cognitions);
D: solving of unconscious conflicts (Dynamics);
E: enabling understanding and communication (Existentials).

In the following, I shall be discussing these elements in greater detail, but one thing needs to be said straightaway. They will not all be of *the same* relevance for *all* patients *throughout* the duration of treatment. Normally, psychotherapeutic treatment begins with the establishment of the therapeutic relationship (A). Respect, interest, empathy, and professional concern form the foundation for supportive and stabilising interactions that hold out hope for the future. This stage is frequently followed by interventions aimed at modifying behaviour (B). Agreement on a particular therapy setting is, in itself, a behavioural offer reassuring patients that it is good and right for them to be dealing actively with their problems and disorders. Whatever school of therapy the therapist comes from, verbal exchange will inevitably and spontaneously offer the patient a model that he or she can learn to engage with. The clarification of dysfunctional attitudes and beliefs (C) also evolves more or less automatically from the therapeutic interview. Different assessments, opinions, and prejudices collide and cease to be "carved in stone". Ideally, the confrontation between the patients' constructions of reality and the scientifically grounded and experience-based opinions of their therapists will lead to salutary insights.

Once the scope for trustful resonance has been established, the time has come to enact unconscious relational conflicts (D). Psychoanalysts refer to this as transference and countertransference. Light can be cast on this by means of a detailed analysis of the therapeutic relationship. One principle common to all schools of psychotherapeutic thought is that patients should be encouraged to enter into a creative dialogue with their environment. Sometimes, this requires only a few sessions; in other cases it might take years of psychotherapeutic support and assistance. It is by no means banal to repeat once again that the basis for almost all variations of psychotherapy is verbal exchange based on understanding. Philosophers and anthropologists agree that understanding and communication are the basis of our existence and, hence, also of the therapeutic encounter (E). I shall enlarge on the various dimensions of the ABCDE model below.

As the case histories indicate, the individual elements of practical and integrative psychotherapy are not uniformly significant in all stages of treatment. The differential and integrative application of different methods can also support diagnosis. With all the five elements available, patients and therapists are in a better position to decide on the level that prolonged therapy (if required) should concentrate on. Whether patients will profit more from a generally supportive, a cognitive–behavioural, a psychoanalytic, or an existential therapeutic approach depends not only on diagnosis, but also on their emotional, cognitive, and emotional resources. Integrative therapy, even in its "brief therapy" form, will quickly reveal what kind of therapy the patient in question is most likely to benefit from. This can then be focused on if a longer course of therapy is indicated. I now turn to the individual elements of integrative psychotherapy and discuss them in greater detail.

A: the therapeutic relationship

Supportive relationships are one of the things that make our lives liveable. They extend from the care lavished on us by our parents to the spheres of kindergarten, school, education and training, and, of course, also include professional relations, friendships, and love relationships. As human beings, we need to be seen and responded to. Infants wither and die if they have no one to sensitively return their gaze. This basic human trait remains with us into high old age. Without fulfilling relationships, the world is empty. Psychotherapeutic relationships are a special case in that they draw systematically on the positive aspects of human intercourse: trust, openness, empathy, understanding, appreciation. A working therapeutic relationship is the basis for any kind of psychotherapeutic success. Empathy and competence are two sides of the same coin.

Psychotherapists are faced with a huge range of psychic illnesses, from minor adjustment disorders to severe anxieties, depressions, personality disorders, and psychoses. At the same time, they act as companions accompanying their patents through existential crises. The roles they are called on to play differ widely. At one and the same time, they are experts, companions, and interlocutors, offering their patients security, recognition, and understanding, in that order.

Personal attachment and adjustment are always of major importance. There are very good practical reasons for this, while others—equally significant—are empirical/psychological and neurobiological (cf. e.g., Fonagy et al., 2005).

However, the creation of a fruitful therapeutic relationship is not all sweetness and light. Like everyday relationships, therapy can be imperilled by emotional and intellectual misunderstandings. Sound training and clinical experience are essential if one is to recognise these misunderstandings and resolve them. Once therapists have learnt to accept their patients emotionally, to understand and support them, the foundations have been laid for the application of specific techniques. Patients frequently have things in common, but each case is different, just as love and friendship exhibit certain almost universal patterns and mechanisms while, at the same time, remaining absolutely unique for those involved. Making a therapeutic relationship work is invariably a creative task. This, of course, does not make it any easier, not least because the process usually involves the interplay of both constructive and destructive forces (Holm-Hadulla, 2013).

The therapeutic alliance is a principle that transcends the differences that divide different schools of therapeutic thought. Empirical research has confirmed that the quality of the therapeutic relationship is a decisive factor in the course taken by therapy. Rogers (1957) refers to genuineness, empathy, and appreciation as the mainstays of a positive therapeutic relationship. Cognitive–behavioural therapists and systemic psychotherapists also stress the significance of the therapeutic alliance (see Lambert, 2013). In existential approaches, authentic encounter has been foregrounded by pioneering proponents such as Yalom (2010). Modern psychoanalysts see it as their central therapeutic concern to elucidate the transference and countertransference responses occurring in the therapeutic relationship. This distinguishes them from other approaches (Kernberg, 2013). Yet, here again, respectful acceptance, empathic interest, and professional concern are the essential prerequisites to which these therapists gear their activities. These concepts are usually only subliminally relevant but in therapeutic crisis situations they can act as a valuable guide. I should like to propose "recognition" as the key term in this context because of the biological, psychological, and philosophical implications it brings with it.

Neurobiological studies (e.g., Kandel, 2012) and attachment research (Bowlby, 1988) indicate how important it is in child development for us to be seen and responded to. For adults, recognition is also an essential health factor (Antonovsky, 1987; Csikszentmihalyi, 1996; Seligman, 2012). The concept of recognition also extends to the realms of the social sciences and cultural studies. In philosophical terms, we find the significance of recognition acknowledged most profoundly by Hegel. The problems bedevilling interdisciplinary consensus on the term and the implications of those problems in psychotherapeutic contexts may prove easier to resolve if we draw on the dialectics of recognition elaborated by Hegel. In his epochal *Phenomenology of Spirit* (1807), he ruminates on the long history of human culture. His conclusion is that the development of individuals and societies is a function of the battle for recognition. Philosophical hermeneutics (Gadamer, 1976; Ricoeur, 1981) also underlines the bio-psycho-social significance of recognition as the foundation for all understanding.

An eloquent testimony to the "recognition principle" is the psychotherapeutic counselling given by Freud to Margarete Walter (Roos, 2006). In 1936, Freud was a well-known but also a controversial figure. Margarete's father took her to see Freud because the Walters' family physician had told them that the eighteen-year-old girl was suffering from a mental illness. Her neighbours considered her "odd" and the merchant opposite was convinced that she was "totally insane". She herself felt lonely and unloved. Her mother had died at her birth and her stepmother was cold and unaffectionate. She also found her father unapproachable. She was closely guarded and not allowed to have any interests of her own.

In her session with Freud, Margarete immediately felt accepted: "He genuinely trained his gaze on me." This was not a reference to diagnostic scrutiny, but to the mindful recognition of Margarete as a person. Once Freud had sent her father into the next room, Margarete became aware of an unprecedented feeling of scope. She felt that this interview with her psychotherapist was the first time in her whole life that she had ever been able to talk about herself. The involvement displayed by this attentive listener enabled her to think out loud about her stepmother's dislike of her. She spoke freely about her father's stern refusal to allow her any girlfriends and complained in no uncertain terms about the boredom of school. She described her loneliness and Freud took an interest in everything she had to disclose. Throughout the interview, Margarete felt "enveloped" by his sympathy. Again and again, he encouraged her to go on talking. She reports that this interest opened something up inside her that no one had ever wanted to see. The salutary effect of this one session was quite definitely a function of recognition. This is an existential dimension of every successful therapeutic encounter and we shall be coming back to it in connection with point "E". The recognition embodied by the therapist's gaze opened up new perspectives for Margarete, and those new perspectives changed her life, not least by enabling her to alter her behaviour, the component I turn to next.

B: modifying behaviour

One of the functions of the cultural techniques encapsulated in myths, religions, and philosophies has always been to regulate behaviour. Apparently, individuals and communities need instructions on how to shape the way they behave. Behavioural research proceeds on the assumption that human behaviour is very largely something we learn. Accordingly, it can be modified by the application of (different) learning principles. Classical and operative conditioning and social learning have been with us for quite some time. Via systematic desensitisation, for example, it is possible to counteract notions associated with fear by setting against them activities irreconcilable with the anxiety response, for instance, relaxation and calm reflection. With different degrees of intensity, techniques of this kind have been widely used throughout history. Problem-focused and disorder-specific modifications can make them very effective indeed.

Social learning is ubiquitous in therapeutic relationships (Bandura, 1982). Attention and recognition on the part of the therapist can act as a crucial social reinforcer, supporting beneficial behaviours such as positive self-utterances, increased self-exploration, or patients' own proposals for behaviour alteration. It is a process that heightens the motivation for change. On the basis of a situational analysis, both the functionality and impedimentary sides of the patient's behaviour are closely examined. Subsequently, therapist and patient go in search of alternative behaviours, which are then rehearsed. Details can be found in the relevant behavioural therapy manuals and textbooks.

Frequently, changes in behaviour become a workable proposition only when the patient is able to imagine them beforehand. Imagination is an important adhesive linking emotions, cognitions, and actions. In the individual case, such fantasies are rarely taken from manuals and textbooks. They take shape in the intersubjective situation existing between the persons involved. Here, they can also be discussed and corrected.

In some instances, therapy will, of course, need to concentrate on unconscious conflicts. Yet, even here, the communication of knowledge and concrete engagement with functional modes of behaviour can be helpful. Imagine a student who has an authority conflict with his father and for that reason neglects his gifts and finds it impossible to study systematically. Why should one not give him effective advice on behaviour? In my experience, this does nothing to impair the quality of psychodynamic work. On the contrary, most patients feel supported by such measures and are far more inclined to trust the therapist and achieve true concentration in working on the conflict. The whole conundrum can be summarised by the rules for productive work that I propose to students and professionals in my book on creativity (2011): accept problems, devise rituals, individualise working techniques, avoid disturbance, create freedom zones.

In therapy, behaviours of this kind can be envisaged jointly, a process that frequently encourages patients to embark on systematic experimentation. Individual sessions can be used to reflect on behaviour, moving on from there to engage with the complexion unconsciously imposed by patients on their relationships, a complexion in which the psychodynamic conflicts become visible. Properly used, different behavioural, psychoanalytic, and systemic approaches will not get in each other's way. In the sessions themselves, the aspects focused on will depend on the needs of the patient and the empathy and skill of the therapist. Ultimately, a joint process of communicative understanding will decide on the things requiring primary attention.

The patients referred to in this book have confirmed that, in some phases of therapy, notably in the early stages, behavioural therapy designed to modify their avoidance strategies is helpful. White-collar worker Wolf had immense difficulty holding his own in challenging verbal encounters. His inhibitions, bouts of depression, and lack of self-esteem made it difficult for him to assert his views. In psychoanalytic terms, it was apparent that this was bound up with ambivalent identification with the father. His unconscious take on the situation was as follows: if I'm successful, I'll be behaving like my Nazi father. Despite these profound conflicts, the following rules proved useful in professional situations where it was necessary to negotiate with others: separate the real from the emotional, focus on interests rather than ideologies, devise options for all parties to the conflict. In my view, discussing rules like these is by no means detrimental, even if the main therapeutic focus is on memories, dreams, and relationship problems.

Sigmund Freud, the founder of psychoanalysis, never shied away from cognitive–behavioural therapy interventions. In the encounter with Margarete Walter referred to earlier, he gave the young woman direct advice on matters of behaviour. Rational discussion of dysfunctional attitudes—a frequent feature of behavioural therapies—was another thing he resorted to, by no means rarely. He told Margarete that she was eighteen and was, therefore, an adult. That meant that she should stop complaining and start developing her own personality. Living up to her own desires would invariably involve disputes with others. If she wanted to assert her own interests, she should not take everything lying down but behave with determination and stalwart resolve. To illustrate this, Freud referred to the cinema outings with her father, who always left the cinema with her when couples started kissing on the screen. Freud advised her to stay put the next time a love scene was shown. This apparently simple behaviour modification operates at many different levels of meaning. From a systemic viewpoint, we would say that it fluidised the relationship. Freud, the therapist, adopted the position of an "auxiliary" ego supporting, reassuring, and encouraging his patient. Probably, much of what Margarete felt to be decisive for the course her life was to take remained unconscious.

This example tells us one important thing: behavioural interventions are invariably linked to intellectual, emotional, and unconscious processes. In the next section, we turn to cognitive engagement with inappropriate concepts of our selves and the world we live in.

C: correcting inappropriate emotional schemas and cognitive concepts

Narratives, myths, religions, philosophies, and scientific truths are all firmly rooted in human behaviour and provide guidance in a confusing, not to say chaotic, world. Cognitive approaches to therapy have grown from these proposals for the way we (should) see the world and the way we (should) lead our lives. Therapists of this persuasion are fond of invoking the Roman philosopher Epictetus, who suggested that it was not events that worried people, but the way they assessed those events. This insight actually goes back even further, underlying Socrates' method of conducting a discussion and the cultural techniques derived from that method. At present, much is also made of Buddhist and Confucian teachings designed to help patients be mindful of their own thoughts and feelings and put them in order. One of the things these approaches quite definitely encourage is the experience of coherence (Holm-Hadulla, 2013).

Cognitive–behavioural therapists concentrate on the systematic modification of dysfunctional patterns of perception, thought, and attitude. This, of course, involves devising alternative views and behaviours. In Beck's version of cognitive therapy (Beck, 1976) and Ellis' rational–emotive behavioural therapy (Ellis, 1980), the assumption is that individuals do not react directly to situations or events. Instead, their conscious or unconscious evaluations of these things are essential for their responses. Distorted evaluations can be rectified via cognitive and experience-based strategies within a constructive alliance. Normally, however, this is not feasible without an appreciation of the unconscious processes that constantly influence our thoughts and feelings. We now have neuroscientific evidence for those processes (e.g., Kandel, 2012).

Accordingly, various forms of behavioural therapy that were initially based entirely on theories of learning now pay much greater heed than before to emotional and unconscious processes. This has led to analogies with psychodynamic and existential therapy procedures. Concepts such as the cognitive–behavioural analysis system of psychotherapy (CBASP) and schema therapy illustrate the degree to which the significance of life experience and its unconscious processing has come to be appreciated (McCullough, 2003; Young et al., 2008). In dialectical–behavioural therapy (Linehan, 2014) we also find an integration of body-orientated and spiritual aspects. Acceptance and commitment therapy (Hayes et al., 1999) also seeks the marriage of long-familiar cultural techniques with modern therapeutic strategies. "Mindfulness" is a key heading under which old cultural techniques are poured into new forms. Psychotherapy, including the cognitive–behavioural variety, has gone holistic. Increasingly, "functional contextualism" has become the watchword, with the focus on the interrelations between patients and their environments. Behaviour is interpreted like a text that is meaningful in a specific situation.

This view is, however, also fundamental to systemic and psychoanalytic approaches. The examples quoted indicate how similar methods that initially appear so different can, in fact, become. Fundamental to them all are concepts of emotional balance, intellectual clarity, and the comprehension of personal life situations against the background of biography and the social world. Opening up perspectives for the future is another aspect that plays a more or less explicit role. The techniques and methods that therapists choose to achieve these objectives should be geared to their patients rather than a school of thought. Some will prefer direct behaviour modification and intellectual reflection. Others are looking for the scope afforded by free association, dreams, and fantasies. And it is by no means rare for this to change in the course of therapy. After an initial phase of support and stabilisation (A), it is frequently necessary to switch to cognitive–behavioural interventions (B and C). Subsequently, the therapeutic process will frequently need to be deepened, opening up spaces for free association and the analysis of unconscious relationship conflicts (D). All this can be readily integrated into an overarching strategy combining understanding, communication, and creativity (E).

D: the dynamics of unconscious psychic processes

A recent example of the integration of various therapeutic approaches is mentalization-based therapy (MBT) (Fonagy et al., 2005). This is a species of psychodynamic therapy that can be readily associated with modern cognitive strategies. MBT proceeds on the assumption that the mentalization of affects and relationship experience is fundamental to psychic health. This is also one of the mainstays of psychoanalytic therapy (Freud, 1914g). Since Freud, psychoanalysis has been rooted in both neuroscientific research and in the great narratives of our culture. To this day, it has remained a blend of natural science, social science, and cultural studies. In the meantime, awareness of unconscious psychic processes, an awareness furthered not least by neurobiological research, has become more or less common knowledge. We may safely assume that most human behaviour is determined by unconscious emotions, information processing routines, and action impulses. We now also have neurobiological confirmation of the effectiveness of working on unconscious conflicts (cf. Kandel, 2012).

From a psychoanalytic perspective, pathological conflicts derive from the interplay between disposition factors and (repeated) traumatic experiences. Defective attachments, offence, disappointments, and abuse can generate any number of physical and mental symptoms. They frequently also interfere with the notions one entertains about oneself and the outside world. These notions and the emotions associated with them can seriously distort reality. They also have an inherent tendency to confirm themselves. This leads not only to misprisions of our own needs and actions, but also to a misguided design for living that is harmful to ourselves and sometimes to others. However, because psychic models of coherence are necessary to impose order on chaotic emotions and cognitions, they are usually highly constant even though they might lead to dissatisfaction and despair. It invariably takes a long stretch of hard (therapeutic) work to replace them with more satisfactory concepts of self and world.

Here, the creative invocation of the past plays a major part. Successful psychodynamic therapy opens up a space in which patients can "play" with memories, ideas, and affects (Winnicott, 1971). This play is not a negation of reality. On the contrary, therapeutic playspace frequently paves the way for a more successful shaping of reality. This can improve substantially the feeling of self-efficacy, normally something that therapists with cognitive–behavioural leanings tend to concentrate on.

In modern psychoanalysis, the fantasies focusing on the relationship with the therapist are given special attention because they are regarded as an iteration of the patient's relational conflicts. Therapists make use of the feelings and ideas triggered in them by their patients to arrive at a better understanding of the inner world those patients inhabit. This makes it possible to work on central relationship conflicts in the here and now of the therapeutic alliance. I would, however, see it as a restricted view of the dimensions operative in therapeutic encounter to consider everything uttered by patients to be an instance of conflictual transference that can only be worked on via analysis of the countertransference. Frequently, consciously facing up to repressed impulses and seeing them in terms of memory, fantasy, and dream will deprive them of their pathological potential and make patients feel more complete. From a psychoanalytic vantage, it is also an existential challenge and a creative task to transform the destructive impulses lurking in every human individual into constructive psychic and social activity (Freud, 1920g, 1933b).

I normally begin therapeutic treatment by demonstrating recognition and sympathy for my patients. At the same time, I attempt to create an interpersonal atmosphere in which patients can devote themselves authentically not only to their concerns and troubles, but also to their hopes and their potential. When I become aware of dysfunctional behaviours, I do my best to address and improve them. I also make direct reference to cognitive schemas that are patently prompting patients to take a misguided view of their internal and external reality. Once the therapeutic process reaches a deeper level, patients usually find spontaneous access to a mood in which they can devote themselves to their creative ideas, fantasies, and dreams. The same thing happens on the therapist's side. Here, fantasies materialise and can point the way to conflict resolution and release creative potential.

In phases of psychoanalytic therapy in which the focus is on transference and countertransference, it can make eminently good sense not to lose sight of the cognitive and behavioural dimensions. Especially when patients entrap themselves in ill-defined fantasies and threaten to lose their bearings, cognitive–behavioural interventions will help to prevent malignant regression. This is especially important with patients threatened by psychotic structure loss.

E: existential creativity

In the eyes of philosophical anthropology, understanding and communication are the foundations of human existence (Gadamer, 1976; Ricoeur, 1981). Even babies actively process the stimuli from their own body and the environment. In fact, it is no metaphorical exaggeration to say that babies "compose" their own worlds. This primary creativity remains potent into high old age, unless it is destroyed by traumatic experiences and illness. Neurobiological studies indicate that the simultaneous arousal of nerve cells creates networks that form the basis for neuronal organisation. Coherent neuronal networks are indispensable for the functionality of an organism (see Holm-Hadulla,

2013). These networks organise our perceptions and condition our memories. Stimuli, affects, and feelings are linked with corresponding thoughts, moods, and experiences to form a complex structure that guarantees a degree of organismic stability. In psychological terms, it is legitimate to refer to this organisation as a psychic structure that forms the basis for a feeling of identity, emotional control, and meaningful activity.

Coherent organisation of experience is a crucial element in cultural formation. Cultural studies scholars such as Assmann (1995) point out that, from the beginning of human history, individuals have communicated with others about themselves and their place in the world by means of myths, religions, and other narratives. Every individual is an integral part of a communicative world. Understanding and communication are not merely technical resources; they are the foundations of human existence. Philosophical anthropologists insist that understanding and communication are modes of being with which human individuals both find the way to their own selves and create a social world. It is important to note that understanding communication need not be verbal. It can also come about via gaze, motion, voice, and physical contact. A multitude of sense impressions gels into a unique encounter. Epistemologically, it is impossible for this complex instance of intersubjective and aesthetic experience to be fully explained in terms of scientific or empirical/psychological categories. Fuchs (2016) has shown that the brain is a relational organ that transmits sociocultural, mental, psychological, and corporeal realities. Brain functions are necessary, but not sufficient, conditions for understanding. Life experience is merely processed by the neurons; they cannot take its place. The significance of experience is the fruit of existential understanding (cf. Holm-Hadulla, 2004).

Psychotherapy of any kind implies existential contact with the meaning of the past, the situation at the moment, and designs for the future. It would be naïve to believe that psychotherapists have better answers to the essential issues of human existence than experienced individuals, philosophers, or artists, but they have learnt to provide their patients with a resonant space in which they can describe their sufferings and engage with them successfully at various levels. If we define creativity as the ability to generate new and usable forms, each of these dimensions involves a creative aspect (cf. Holm-Hadulla, 2013). The handling of the therapeutic relationship is, in itself, a cooperative creative process normally generating new and frequently pertinent experiences (A). One can also legitimately refer to coping with individual avoidance behaviour and discovering alternative behaviours as creative activities. The same applies to the development of new attitudes and conflict solutions (C, D). In the last analysis, these individual techniques will have their most beneficial effect when they engender existential understanding and creative communication in an authentic encounter (E).

Existential understanding and creative communication are concepts forged by philosophical anthropology (cf. Gadamer, 1976; Ricoeur 1981). It elaborated hermeneutics as a universal art of understanding. It serves well as an overarching theory within which individual therapeutic techniques can be differentially applied as the disorder requires. Its key reference points are history, language, and subjective experience. "Historicality" means that we are all part of an historical and social development that determines the way we think and feel. This is why all psychotherapeutic schools of thought take an interest in patients' memories. Only at a distance vouchsafed by history can we understand earlier experience. In the process of understanding, that experience becomes comprehensible at one remove. Psychotherapy can help us to take possession of our own histories and feel more complete as a result. This is where the second pillar of hermeneutics comes into its own: language.

For hermeneutic thinkers, language encompasses all forms of human expression, not just verbal exchange, but also music, art, dance, facial expression, and gesture. As humans, we have no choice but to express ourselves. In connection with "recognition", we have seen that being seen and responded to is a fundamental human need. This need makes use of language in all its different forms. Yet, language is not a mere tool or utensil, it is a compendium of experience that we are born into. Language envelops us and "earths" us. We find our way around in the world via language. Our affects turn into tangible feelings when they have found expression.

The third key term in hermeneutics is intersubjective experience. Gadamer (1976) and Ricoeur (1981) tell us that genuine understanding is the fruit of shared experience. The case reports in this book demonstrate how new and useful creative ideas materialise in the therapeutic encounter. These ideas can express themselves as a visual image, a musical memory, or some other kind of sense impression.

When a trusting therapeutic alliance has come about, patients will trigger in their therapists ideas, fantasies, and moods that they can give back to the patients in a new and understandable form. This is a part of what modern psychotherapists refer to as "mentalization": understanding feelings, thoughts, and modes of experience in a process of dynamic intersubjectivity.

Understanding the meaning of experiences improves our feeling of coherence and self-efficacy and, accordingly, our sense of reality. The experience gained in this way is never complete, it opens out on to a horizon for new experiences. This view of understanding as intrinsically incomplete dialogic activity can look back on a long tradition. It is embodied not only in Western philosophy by figures such as Plato, but also in the great oriental traditions: for example, by Confucius.

Different as they are, all the patients described in this book were able to experience the salutary effect of dialogic understanding at first hand. It led to a creative transformation of their mood swings, anxieties, and relationship problems. Creative transformation takes place when diffuse affects and confusing thoughts find expression in feelings, memories, fantasies, and dreams and, thus, become comprehensible. In psychological terminology, we might refer to this as an increase in emotional and cognitive coherence. Neuroscientific and psychological studies indicate that this psychotherapeutic principle transcends the various schools of thought (cf. Holm-Hadulla, 2013). However, asked to name an overarching theory encompassing them all, I would still refer to the art of hermeneutic understanding because it includes historical and cultural experiences. By means of trusting communication, we acquire familiarity with, and recognition of, our world.

Margarete Walter said that the interview with Freud "opened" her and "let her become". He provided a decisive impulse and released her into "the liberty to go wherever she wanted" (Roos, 2006). My patients found out that it normally takes a long time for psychotherapy to trigger such a creative process. They confirm (indirectly) that creative encounter with oneself and one's environment is a principle that unites the schools of thought we referred to earlier. It is a foundation on which we can integrate various psychotherapeutic techniques in a unique encounter. Symptoms fade and zest is restored to life, both clear indications that self and world have found their way back to a creative exchange.

For psychotherapeutic training, the implications of what we have been saying are manifold. Very often, psychotherapists, doctors, and people in other professions practise psychotherapy for years before completing their training in one of the recognised therapeutic procedures. At the outset, in particular, the integrative psychotherapy model can provide them with a general guideline. Naturally, full training in one of the recognised techniques is indispensable for people with severe disorders. None the less, even at the outset, this never entitles us to ignore the insights that other procedures have come up with. It makes very good sense for, say, psychodynamic and psychoanalytic training candidates to attend classes on cognitive–behavioural and systemic approaches. The same applies equally *vice versa*, of course. Depending on what came first, one could speak here of integrative behavioural therapy, integrative psychodynamic therapy, or integrative psychoanalysis. Equally indispensable is familiarity with disorder-specific and psychiatric concepts and strategies, as well as the fundamentals of psychosomatic medicine.

These theories and practical instructions serve as a basis for structuring the psychotherapeutic landscape and taking account of various therapeutic procedures. In case discussions, different methods can be tailored to specific situations, always bearing in mind the relevant societal and cultural parameters. All this flows together in a unique encounter that not only does away with distressful symptoms, but also encourages personal and social development. It is anything but a luxury if, in therapy, we keep a close eye on the existential and creative progress of our patients, rather than concentrating exclusively on disorder-specific approaches and closely defined methods. As we have seen in the case vignettes, this progress is a crucial psychotherapeutic factor.

For therapists, reflection on their experience of life is just as important because of the effect such experience has on any kind of psychological assessment. This happens not only in psychotherapeutic self-experience, but also in active participation in life itself. Cultural experiences are very much a part of this. Literature, cinema, music, and art bestow on us experiences and insights beyond the scope of neuroscientific and psychological methods. Accordingly, artistic portrayals of psychic disorders and the engagement with them are indispensable sources of psychotherapeutic education. An outstanding example is the life and work of scientist, statesman, and poet Johann

Wolfgang von Goethe (Holm-Hadulla, 2017). He shows us how anxieties, bouts of depression, and bewildering passions can be coped with by means of understanding, communication, and creativity and transformed into dynamic health. At the end of the poem "Blissful Longing", written after many painful experiences, Goethe tells us how essential it is to see life as a creative transformation of pain. Deeply influenced by Eastern cultures, the European resumes:

> And so long as you do not have it,
> this "die and become!"
> you will only be a gloomy guest
> on the dark earth.

REFERENCES

Antonovsky, A. (1987). *Unraveling the Mystery of Health: How People Manage Stress and Stay Well.* San Francisco, CA: Jossey-Bass.

Assmann, J. (1995). Collective memory and cultural identity.*New German Critique, 65*: 125–133.

Bandura, A. (1982). Self efficacy mechanism in human agency. *American Psychologist, 37*: 122–147.

Beck, A. T. (1976). *Cognitive Therapy and the Emotional Disorders.* New York: International Universities Press.

Bowlby, J. (1988). *A Secure Base.* London: Routledge.

Csikszentmihalyi, M. (1996). *Creativity.* New York: HarperCollins.

Ellis, A. (1980). Rational emotive psychotherapy and cognitive behavior therapy: similarities and differences. *Cognitive Therapy and Research, 4*: 325–340.

Feixas, G., & Botella, L. (2004). Psychotherapy integration: reflections and contributions from a constructivist epistemology. *Journal of Psychotherapy Integration, 14*: 192–222.

Fonagy, P., Gergely, G., Jurist, E., & Target, M. (2005). *Affect Regulation, Mentalization, and the Development of Self.* New York: Other Press.

Frank, J. (1991). *Persuasion and Healing* (3rd edn). Baltimore, MD: Johns Hopkins University Press.

Freud, S. (1914g). Remembering, repeating and working-through. *S. E., 12*: 145–156. London: Hogarth.

Freud, S. (1920g). *Beyond the Pleasure Principle. S. E., 18*: 7–64. London: Hogarth.

Freud, S. (1933b). Why war? *S. E., 18*: 197–215. London: Hogarth.

Fuchs, T. (2016). The brain—a relational organ. *Journal of Consciousness Studies, 18*: 196–221.

Gadamer, H. G. (1976). *Philosophical Hermeneutics*. D. E. Linge (Trans. & Ed.). Berkeley: University of California Press.

Hayes, S. C., Strosahl, K. D., & Wilson, K. G. (1999). *Acceptance and Commitment Therapy: An Experiential Approach to Behavior Change*. New York: Guilford Press.

Hegel, G. W. F. (1807). *Phenomenology of Spirit*. Oxford: Oxford University Press, 1979.

Holm-Hadulla, R. M. (2003). Psychoanalysis as a creative act of shaping. *International Journal of Psychoanalysis, 84*: 1203–1220.

Holm-Hadulla, R. M. (2004). *The Art of Counselling and Psychotherapy*. London: Karnac.

Holm-Hadulla, R. M. (2011). *Kreativität zwischen Schöpfung und Zerstörung* [*Creativity between Construction and Destruction*]. Göttingen: Vandenhoeck & Ruprecht.

Holm-Hadulla, R. M. (2013). The dialectic of creativity: towards an integration of neurobiological, psychological, socio-cultural and practical aspects of the creative process. *Creativity Research Journal, 25*(3): 1–7.

Holm-Hadulla, R. M. (2017). *Passion: The Path to Creativity of the Statesman, Scientist, and Poet Goethe*. London: Karnac.

Kandel, E. R. (2012). *The Age of Insight*. New York: Random House.

Kernberg, O. F. (2013). *Internal World and External Reality*. New York: Jason Aronson.

Lambert, M. (2013). *Bergin and Garfield's Handbook of Psychotherapy and Behavior Change* (6th edn). New York: John Wiley.

Lazarus, A. (1981). *The Practice of Multimodal Therapy*. New York: McGraw-Hill.

Linehan, M. M. (2014). *DBT Skills Training Manual* (2nd edn). New York: Guilford Press.

McCullough, J. P. (2003). *Treatment of Chronic Depression: Cognitive Behavioral Analysis System of Psychotherapy* (*CBASP*). New York: Guilford Press.

Orlinsky, D. E., & Howard, K. I. (1987). A generic model of psychotherapy. *Journal of Integrative and Eclectic Psychotherapy, 6*: 6–27.

Ricoeur, P. (1981). *Hermeneutics and the Human Sciences*. Cambridge: Cambridge University Press.

Rogers, C. R. (1957). *Client-Centered Therapy. First Current Practice, Implications, and Theory*. Boston, MA: Houghton Mifflin.

Roos, P. (2006). Der große Zuhörer. *DIE ZEIT, 18*: 1–5.

Seligman, M. (2012). *Flourish: A Visionary New Understanding of Happiness and Well-Being*. New York: Atria Books.

Wampold, B. E. (2007). Psychotherapy: the humanistic (and effective) treatment. *American Psychologist, 62*: 857–873.

Winnicott, D. W. (1971). *Playing and Reality*. London: Tavistock.

Yalom, I. D. (2010). *Existential Psychotherapy* (5th edn). New York: Basic Books.

Young, J. E., Klosko, J. S., & Weishaar, H. E. (2008). *Schema Therapy. A Practitioner's Guide*. New York: Guilford Press.

INDEX